Between a Rock and a Hard Place

BETWEEN
A ROCK
AND
A HARD
PLACE

Edited by
Deaf Ex-Mainstreamers Group (DEX)

Published in 2003 by
Deaf Ex-Mainstreamers Group
Evans Business Centre
Monckton Road
Wakefield
West Yorkshire WF2 7AS

© 2003   Deaf Ex-Mainstreamers Group

ISBN 0-9546699-0-8

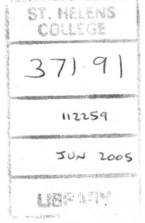

Cover design by The Attic Design Studio, Kings Norton, Birmingham B30 3JN

Design and typesetting by John Saunders Design and Production, OX13 5HU
Printed in Great Britain by Biddles Ltd, King's Lynn

Contents

Contents

Definition of "deaf"

The use of the capital D is used throughout the book to represent those Deaf people who identify with, and are accepted by, the British Sign Language using Deaf community.

Lower case d symbolises non-signing deaf people or is used generically for all deaf people.

Dedication

"Dedicated in memoriam to Robert Oakes, and all those who have died and suffered because of deaf mainstream education."

Foreword by Dr Colin Baker

Colin Baker is Professor of Education at the University of Wales, Bangor, Director of Research Centre Wales, a Fellow of the British Psychological Society and a member of the Welsh Language Board (a Governmental Language Planning Department.)

His books include Aspects of Bilingualism in Wales (1985), Key Issues in Bilingualism and Bilingual Education (1988), Attitudes and Language (1992) Foundations of Bilingual Education and Bilingualism (1993, second edition 1996, third edition 2001), and the Encyclopaedia of Bilingualism and Bilingual Education(1998 co-authored with Sylvia Prys Jones). Editor of the International Journal of Bilingual Education and Bilingualism.

Deaf people and bilinguals have much in common. In times past, both groups have been seen as having disabilities, deficiencies and disadvantages. Bilinguals, for example, have previously been labelled mentally retarded and schizophrenic purely for having two languages. But in recent decades, there has been a growing realisation of the many advantages of owning two languages, and of being bicultural.

Deaf people have, over time, found a parallel with bilinguals. There is increasing recognition of, and status for sign language, once a symbol of oppression, but now seen as giving full communication and cognitive possibilities. Increasingly, Deaf people are included as one group of minority language bilinguals. Having sign plus literacy and/or oracy in another language creates bilingualism. Thus Deaf bilinguals can share the advantages now known to exist among bilinguals. Some of these advantages are regarded as:

- Increased cognitive development
- Greater mental flexibility and ability to think more abstractly
- Lateral and creative thinking
- Metalinguistic awareness – bilinguals respond to word/ sign meaning
- Social and economic diversity

- Ability to move between two languages and language communities – biculturalism
- For deaf children, sign language acts as a bridge towards the acquisition of spoken language (either literacy and / or oracy.)

However, languages within individuals and society do not just thrive by themselves. Like with ecological conservation, we have to protect the smaller, rarer species. All minority languages, including sign languages, need protection and language planning. Such planning starts with persuading parents to use the minority language with the child so that bilingualism in the minority and the majority language becomes possible. Bilingual education which uses both languages in content teaching further enables bilingualism, and then literacy and / or oracy can occur for deaf people. In many cases, such bilingualism and literacy leads to biculturalism. But for parents to speak a minority language to their child, and for schools to teach through a minority language, there has to be economic, leisure, social and cultural uses for that language beyond the home and the school gates. There has to be instrumental and integrative purposes for a language to survive through the teenage years, into adulthood and to flourish throughout life. Therefore, there has to be opportunities for a minority language to be used not only in social and leisure activity, but ideally also in finding employment, earning a salary and getting promotion. A language without a language economy may be in danger in the future.

Among Deaf people there has been the redefinition of Deaf identity, a drive for empowerment, increasing recognition of the right to self ownership of their own destiny, a distinctiveness in their community and cultural life, and the generation of needed assertiveness, action, and ambition. This book valuably serves that drive forward, that movement into the future where the advantages for Deaf bilinguals are increasingly recognised and celebrated.

Colin Baker
2003

Introduction

This book is an essential source of information for all who are deaf, and who live and work with deaf people, because so little is known about the effects of normalisation on deaf people, via mainstreaming in hearing schools, or monolingualism (spoken language only) in Deaf schools. This type of communication is often called "oralism" but because of the ambiguity of the term we prefer the plain –speak of just spoken language. We hope this will emphasise the lack of status of possessing just one language, even though sign language is incorrectly viewed by many as being an inferior language. It is a well researched fact that there are many benefits of being bilingual in terms of both social and economic diversity.

The Deaf Ex-Mainstreamers' Group (DEX) was established because of our concerns that those who had been wholly or partly through this system, are in limbo between the worlds of hearing and deaf people, and there is growing evidence that deaf people are struggling in the hearing communities, despite the best intentions of hearing professionals to integrate us. "Between a Rock and a Hard Place" is testimony to this, as deaf mainstreamers (some still in school) have described so eloquently and movingly. Several accounts also describe life at monolingual Deaf schools, where sign language is not permitted, but mostly write warmly about the fellowship there is with deaf peers.

DEX has collected the stories, papers and articles – all written by deaf people – together in the hope that our message will be used to change the deaf education system to one that is sign bilingual for all deaf children, regardless of levels of hearing loss, and for all deaf children to be placed together, either in mainstream resourced schools or in Deaf schools which all use sign bilingualism. Furthermore, DEX wants hearing children to learn sign language too, as a vocational subject, or for interest, but primarily for friendship and understanding of deaf people's needs.

The experiences recounted in the book are of abuse, mostly through ignorance and neglect and sometimes through misuse of power, and we know of deaf young people who have taken their lives because of their treatment in schools. This book is dedicated to Robert Oates, who sadly committed suicide recently. Because of this collective evidence, there is need for action.

Although the breakthrough is hard, DEX is working towards being part of the policy making infrastructure to include deaf children's needs in government decisions and to supporting those who already have good practice in deaf education, from our perspective as Deaf Users. We want to work with other Deaf –led organisations towards our pool of expertise being utilised in leadership within deaf education, building on the Deaf community's powerful drive to gain recognition of British Sign Language by the Government. Also for deaf people who are on the fringe of the Deaf Community to be welcomed and included by Deaf people, whilst serious discussion is given to the oppressive practice of labelling with D/d.If all deaf children are sign bilingual then there can be no devisiveness and all children will be proud Ds, sure of their Deaf identities and their places in the world. There is, therefore, some hope for parents and families of deaf children, if full information about the benefits of sign bilingualism is given during their child's early years, and support is both consistent and ongoing.

Colin Baker, an internationally respected professor of language planning and bilingualism has written a Foreword for this book to show its importance in terms of information and deaf people's need for bilingualism.

However, there is still need for more anecdotal information from the countless other deaf mainstreamed and monolingual Deaf school pupils in the U.K. and internationally. If you wish to comment on "Between a Rock and a Hard Place", readers are encouraged to contact DEX via our website, and to come forward as a sign of solidarity and support in a campaign to make real and lasting changes for deaf children and their futures.

Acknowledgements

We are very grateful to each and all who have contributed for their excellent work. The deaf writers and poets have struggled to express themselves in the face of difficulties with spoken language, and also to reveal deep seated and traumatic experiences, sometimes having to analyse feelings that may never have been allowed to surface before. Without their courage to "speak out" DEX could not have achieved this piece of work.

Furthermore, we want to thank all who have painstakingly put the items together: in particular, David Leach, Cynthia Stringer, Steve Emery, Mickey Fellowes, Jill Jones and Janet Hansborough for her usual capable administration support. Further thanks must go to Peter Jackson, Forest Bookshop and Ian Randell in their advice on general layout. Also, Colin Baker for so kindly giving up valuable time to write the Foreword and for meeting us to clarify bilingual, multi-lingual and language planning issues.

The publishing of "Between a Rock and a Hard Place" could not have materialised without funding from the Community Fund, as part of the Best Value Review project, and to them we are deeply grateful.

Finally, we want our families and friends, DEX members and Committee members who all offered encouragement and interest to know that we appreciate their support.

1

Making the transition to being deaf

An extra-terrestrial view

In order to obtain a more detached view of this subject I tried to imagine what beings from another planet make of the situation for the group of congenitally or early deafened children and adults. They would find a number of factors. The most startling one would be that only a small proportion of this particular group are able to communicate fluently with each other, whilst the larger remainder communicate in another language which is difficult for them to acquire and to use and which they, mainly, use with non-deaf people. Martians may see that deaf people cannot easily understand each other by using the language of hearing people and may need interpreters.

Martians may note that the smaller grouping is cohesive because they meet regularly, enjoy a full social calendar, take real effort and pride in their language and culture and enjoy being who they are. They would note the significance of the capital D for culturally Deaf people. On the other hand there are congenitally deaf people who do not, on the whole, meet up and when they do, feel that they are not, or cannot be, "big D's" (because "big D's" do not accept "small d's").

Oralism and technology – the great dividers

Some speculation by the Martians may then lead on to why this has happened. Who or what divides those born deaf or early deafened children? They decided that it begins with people measuring how much hearing the child is thought to have and then attempting to give as much back as possible. The Martians, skilled in making highly sophisticated technology, were astounded that the technical devices, called hearing aids or cochlear implants and their usage in education (auralism) do not restore full hearing, so that the children are still deaf; although they can obviously hear better than without the aids. Some children are naturally viewed as being hearing children once these devices are worn.

The Martians' sensitive antennae could ascertain that the hearing aids are noisy, with unnatural and poor quality sounds. Sometimes the sounds are too intrusive and startle the wearers. Background noises merge with direct one-to-one communication, and there is no sense of direction of where sound comes from. Ear moulds and aids are often uncomfortable; the aids are stress-making when worn for long periods. Making sense of sounds is like doing a permanent auditory crossword puzzle without pen and paper. Despite all these drawbacks, children and adults may wear them with no compulsion and can feel deprived without them.

Cochlear implants give even less information for the wearer to make sense of. There are more wires and apparatus as well as part of it being surgically implanted in the head. Both types of aids have not been researched comprehensively, except for auditory gain and to make refinements. No account has been taken of the effects on the mind and body of listening through unnatural devices or any long term side effects such as stress-related illnesses, tinnitus or recruitment.

Martians may note that without many auditory clues, deaf children have to make even more use of visual clues, hence the reason for the attachment to auditory technical devices on the part of many deaf people (although profoundly Deaf adults state that visual technology is more relevant to their culture). Sign language is favoured over spoken language/body language-reading (or lip-reading as it is inappropriately called).

Deaf people who use spoken language often ask hearing people to become their non-technical "hearing aid". Martians may notice how aggressive hearing people become when asked to change their behaviour, modulate their spoken language or to learn a second language. It is seen to be unhearing-like to act in this way. It could only be because deafness is viewed as being inferior so hearing people do not like to behave in deaf fashion, even in private.

The visual crossword puzzle, again without pen or paper (lip-reading) is tiring and stressful. It may be noted by the Martians' strumming antennae that, for younger deaf children and people whose stamina is still good and whose energy replacement levels are high, tiredness is far less of a problem than it is for deaf adults.

What is hard to understand, as a Martian (and indeed, as a Deaf person) is why hearing people consider that deaf children can function in the same way as hearing children in hearing schools? The word "cope" is used a lot. The other great mystery is why, if older deaf children and deaf adults are able to give account of their experiences, why those responsible for the education and well-being of deaf children are, in the main, unable to accept these accounts as said in Anon (2000).

Resistance to change is one factor: no-one likes to feel that one's training and work efforts have been counter-productive. Why, then, can't Deaf people train hearing professionals to ensure that training is more effective? Deaf people must obviously be underprivileged and the concept behind helping underprivileged people is that privileged helpers must appear to know more, otherwise there is equal status. "Interesting!" bleep the Martians – who, of course, have had an equal opportunities policy for thousands of years. Now that we have the extra-terrestrial comments, how do we proceed? With transitions in big and small steps.

Status within the Deaf community

When the Deaf Ex-Mainstreamers' Group (DEX) was inaugurated it was aimed primarily at deaf members of the society who are marginalised between the Deaf and hearing cultures. This is as a result of the fragmentation caused by oralism and technology; it has created minorities within our minority group, differing cultures, languages and communication systems, attitudes and behaviour, leading to aggression and conflict towards one another. Discrimination is rife amongst deaf people.

At present we have these descriptions of differing identity groups: hard of hearing (used to be only applied to adventitiously deafened adults, but confusingly, some deaf children are called this); hearing impaired; partially hearing; partially deaf; profoundly deaf; stone deaf; oral (which includes "think-hearing" or "hearing focus"); half deaf; not really deaf; deafened; deaf or deaf; deaf and the now contentious word "dumb"; born deaf or born hearing and then became deaf; big D or small d.

DEX is a half-way house, or stepping stones – depending on how deaf people wish to use it – to encourage members to positively access their identity and to actively support each other in understanding themselves as deaf people. It is hoped that it can act as a catalyst to enable those who were brought up as "think-hearing" people to develop as deaf or Deaf people.

It must be hard for hearing and Deaf people to understand that deaf people cannot become Deaf overnight. Even if all Deaf community members actively welcomed non-signing deaf people into their midst they still say that deaf people must have a "good attitude". Close examination of this phenomena, I hope, will explain why it is not possible to achieve this instantly.

Taking first the analogy of the onion to represent the broader deaf community, the core of the onion is the core of the BSL Deaf community. The rings that fan outwards represent those who are on the fringes of the Deaf community, starting with those who don't attend Deaf clubs or regular meetings but who identify with the culture, to those who are think-hearing. Those on the outer rings of the skin of the onion may feel rejected and unwanted. The onion analogy is not an equal opportunities model but it reflects the current divisions.

I prefer the example of an orange, rich in diversities and which all play an equal part in the deaf community. The d/D criteria, although used in describing identities is also damning. As one deaf friend said: "I had grown a thick skin in dealing with bad attitudes from hearing people but I did not expect to be treated in such a way by my own kind by being called small d."

Being called hearing, sign-like-hearing, look-like-hearing, not really deaf, oral or small d are cruellest insults of the worst kind to deaf people who are struggling to make sense of their deafness. It is understandable that Deaf people remember the "oral successes" in their Deaf schools being wheeled out to be shown off to visitors and backlash against deaf people who venture into their Deaf clubs. Until Nirvana arrives, there will be different groupings as described, or until oralism and technology can be used to our advantage and not as division-makers. The aim should be for all deaf people to belong to one "orange" or circle, with different segments or parts. Non-signing deaf people need understanding as to why they feel more like hearing people than deaf people and should be encouraged to participate in Deaf cultural activities.

Any broad community should allow for small groupings to occur as this is natural human behaviour. Being brought up in the hearing communities, Deaf people come from all backgrounds, religions, sexual orientations, gender, races and ethnic groups and have diverse interests so it is to be expected that there are a vast range of interest and identity groups in the Deaf community. It is important to allow deaf people who are finding their identity to belong too and they should not be seen as a threat to the existence of the common group. It would also be kinder to view the small d group as learners, not as aliens.

Think-hearing

It is no-one's fault that deaf children are often not given permission to be Deaf. The hearing system opts to "auditorise" and normalise them. Lane (1983). It is flying against nature to force people to be what they are not. Using residual hearing usefully is one thing, rejecting one's identity is another.

Deaf children are born to hearing parents in 90% of cases. Identity formation begins at birth as children model their behaviour on their parents and other family members. As R.D. Laing (1969) states, 'We learn to be who we are told we are'

Hearing parents always check that their baby is free from disability at birth. Unless there is reason to believe otherwise, deafness is usually not diagnosed until at least eight months onwards in which time a routine has been established. Bonding has been based on parent/baby talk and rapport through the common 'hearing ness' they have. There may be suspicions that there is something different happening and the diagnosis may even come as a relief, especially if there has been difficulty in convincing professionals that their baby is behaving differently. However, after diagnosis, hearing parents may be in shock and grieving for the child that is no longer the same as them.

Hearing professionals often go to great lengths to minimise the differences in attempts to placate parents that there is nothing wrong. As hearing people they will obviously identify with how parents feel, without consideration of how the deaf child can form a unique identity, given to the child at birth or soon after. This is how Deaf adults/professionals, working with hearing professionals, can help the family to find its equilibrium.

Deaf children have to learn how to be Deaf. Having only hearing people to identify with means that, despite having wires and receivers emanating from one's head, by some magical process one is a hearing person. Obviously, the more residual hearing a child has, the more likely she will feel she is a hearing person. In other words "think-hearing" Higgins (1990). I am aware that in the States this term is an abusive one. I do not use it pejoratively but as a way of describing what is felt. It is an apt term, for, if one has never heard in the same way as hearing people, then how can one know that one is not hearing? The term 'hard of hearing' suggests that it is hard to hear but, in contrast, there is no explanation of how it is 'hard-to-be-deaf' against the background of living constantly with hearing people.

Always plan or 'always calculate'

Deaf Americans also use the term 'always plan' to signify how deaf people who live in the hearing world always have to be on their toes watching out for what comes next. For example, one can often imagine what is being said by getting the gist of the addressee's sentence and even finish the sentence before it is completed. High achievements indeed! The American English meaning of 'plan' may be slightly different from ours. Deaf people are not just planning ahead but also taking account of what has already been said and also what is currently happening (e.g. the host is getting up from the table so this must mean he is asking for a dance?). This takes a huge toll on the deaf person, constantly on 'red alert', concentrating, neck tensed, eyes ever watchful, listening hard if possible, straining for clues from facial expressions and gestures, context and so on. This 'always calculate state' never ends and continues through life, a treadmill where one is competing to understand and keep up, like a hamster caught in its play wheel.

Attitudes towards language

The final term used by ASL using Deaf people is 'mind rich', to signify those deaf people who come from hearing middle-class or wealthy families, who cannot come to terms with the use of sign language, viewed as it is as a second rate language or even as a communication method.

In Britain particularly, there is the prevailing attitude that the English language is the best one in the world, that it is a world wide language and there is no need to resort to another. British people are, in the main, monolingual, unlike our European counterparts. Against this background it is harder than in Sweden, which has a successful bilingual programme for deaf children, to implement the belief that bilingualism is good, especially when sign language is still not recognised here as a language. Being able to sign does not raise a deaf child's status but can even denote to hearing people, and to the child, that this child is failing. There is more status in being monolingual in spoken language.

Immersed as the families of 'mind rich' deaf people are in all the aspects of auditory culture, it is hard for them to make the adjustment to a visual culture, i.e. literature, the arts, music, politics, philosophy, etc., all rely heavily on listening and spoken language.

Deaf and hearing socialisation

In addition to understanding individual needs for change is the need to recognise culture shock. Making the transition from one culture to another always requires adjustment and commitment. According to Adrian Furnham et al (1979) the best way to make the transition is by sojourners being trained in the culture of the new country before leaving to live there and being guided by friendly natives once they arrive.

There is no real difference between the example of sojourners adapting to a new culture and that of hearing family members learning to incorporate their new deaf baby and how to incorporate themselves to their deaf child. Moving from auditory to visual culture requires making vast changes.

Penelope Leach, (1974) child development expert, once said that parents of a new baby asked her how long it would take to 'get back to normal'. Her reply was that life changes once there is a baby in the family and things can never be the same. So it is for hearing parents of deaf babies, except that they have to make a second transition at diagnosis of deafness.

At present, hearing parents are largely left to work out what changes they need to make, depending on a number of factors: how much hearing the child is perceived to have; how much parents want to accept that their child is deaf and how much support they are given to enable them to come to terms with their loss; how much parents understand about deafness; how much information and support is given to the family; how important it is seen to give time and effort to changing to meet the family's needs; how much support is given to them in making the transition from being a hearing family to a hearing/deaf family; how positively deafness is portrayed to the family, and so on.

Identity formation and depersonalisation

Whilst recognising hearing family members' need to be supported through cultural transition, it is also essential to consider how to teach the deaf child to be Deaf. Lack of identity results in poor self image and even in depersonalisation, which in turn can lead to mental illness. Identity, according to R.D. Laing (1969), can take many forms. The two central ones are 'being-for-oneself' and 'being-for-others'. 'Being-for-oneself' is achieved through constant reassurance and praise from the carers, the family, then the extended family and the wider environment. If the child tries to 'be-for-others' at the expense of 'being-for-oneself' the child does not establish real self-esteem on which to build self-confidence and strength of selfhood in later life. If hearing parents desperately want their deaf child to be a quasi-hearing child, the deaf child tries to be hearing for them. As Laing also says, 'The other by his or her actions may impose on self an unwanted identity'.

These conflicting messages mean that the deaf child may deny that she is deaf as she tries to 'be-for-others'. Hearing parents rightly say that deaf children have to live in the hearing world and should learn from an early age how to communicate effectively with hearing people and belong to the society. There can be no disputing this, since deaf people need to have economic security and employment in the society in which they live. However, in contrast it is also important that deaf children can be with others of their own kind and be fluent in the language of their community, otherwise they are marginalised. Any group is uncomfortable when non-native members join the group, not simply because they are new to the group's customs but because communication is not as clear, nor as relaxed. Edwards (1985).

Leaving deaf children's socialisation into the adult Deaf community until adolescence and young adulthood means that a culture shock takes place later for them rather than for their hearing parents. But, because hearing parents are not involved, it is often trivialised. For some reason it is assumed that because sign language is the natural language for deaf people that they will learn it overnight and will, magically, fit into the Deaf club or deaf youth clubs with no hiccups. Any second language takes at least three years to learn, for learners to be fluent.

People who are unclear about their identities or who want to change identities, often need extensive counselling; transsexuals and alcoholics are but two of many examples. Why, then, are deaf adolescents often given a passport to 'Deaf land' after a childhood of being 'think-hearing'? Or, if deaf adults try to brave it out for themselves, they cannot make the transition? Apart from the difficulties of adapting to their own culture, they may find the reactions from hearing family and friends hard to bear – no longer seen as one of them or seen as defectors, ungrateful for their kindness and the 'good' education they have received, etc.

Deaf child-centred education

The education setting is also where identity formation takes place. Learning to be Deaf is not easy if there are no deaf children with whom to identify. It is like looking through a two-way mirror, as one deaf child recognises the other deaf child, they can both see that they are deaf. Their common identities forge them into acceptance of each other just as group members bond into a group. Knowing that one is not alone is also vital to a child's sense of security, which is a basic human need.

Knowing also that others understand adds meaning to life – a second basic human need. Amongst many other factors is also the need for self esteem and self confidence which is reinforced by support from others in the same position. Children will achieve far more academically if they are confident and value themselves. It obviously makes sense to then place a group of deaf children together who are of the same ages and year bands in one school than to place individually (which is becoming more widely favoured).

Mainstream schools must adopt a whole-schools approach to incorporate both hearing and deaf children if they wish for themselves to be truly bicultural and bilingual school. Only then can both deaf children and hearing children benefit from being educated and playing together. This requires governmental funding, LEA's commitment, the school's full understanding of aims and objectives and the will to succeed on behalf of staff and pupils.

The role of professionals

We return now to the role professionals and Deaf adults have in helping families and deaf children to make transitions. However, professionals may need to re-examine their own views on deafness. According to Zen Buddhist masters, the only constancy is change. We all need to accept change and understand its importance to human growth and development. No-one can resist change for, like water, it will find its way around the stones and rocks of life.

Social workers with deaf people and Deaf adults have a crucial role to play at the diagnosis of deaf children and beyond. As the Children Act 1989 and Education Act 1992 both call for more involvement of other agencies apart from educational, it is important that deaf children and their families have access to as much information and support as possible. The vital information about cultural identity can only come, at present, from those who are Deaf or who work with Deaf adults. The Children Act 1989 talks of meeting the cultural and linguistic needs of children (Section 64(3)). How many social services departments are implementing this with respect to all deaf children?

The two above mentioned acts emphasise parent partnerships and close liaison between agencies. It is imperative that this happens and is not tokenistic. Some local authorities are leading the way already. Suffolk, Warwickshire, Bristol and Leeds, to name but a few. However, are all deaf children included in their programmes?

Hopefully, the way will be paved for all deaf children to learn their identities, not just those who are profoundly deaf.

Conclusion

I am, for the first time in my life, in the happy position of knowing that I am not alone in what I think. DEX group members are vocal to their dissatisfaction of the way they have been treated and how to ensure that other deaf children and adults are not treated in the same way. A good education is not enough. Hard won confidence has taken most of us a lifetime. The group has given me already, after less than a year's inauguration, the confidence to write this article as a testimony to others' experiences as well as my own. May the onion make the transition to an orange soon. With the will to learn and change and close liaison between deaf adults, professionals and hearing families, this is the only way transition can be achieved.

Jill Jones
1996

My SIGN

The silent hand moves slowly with grace
then bursts with excitement and quickens the pace
Images drawn with precision in air
with energetic passion, beauty and flair
Saying so much more than the spoken word
A language of generations, never to be heard
The magnet just drew me, it all seemed to fit
sparking powerful emotions – the flame had been lit
Just like the return to a well loved home
no longer on the outside feeling alone
No more incomprehension, struggling to see
what people are saying – I've now found the key
I've unlocked the door and found what I'd lost
I'm staying right here, whatever the cost!
A new freedom of speech to express what I feel
with meaning and depth, in a language that's real
This is what matters, now I feel I can shine
As I show to the world my language, my sign...

Kate Wheat

2   A personal account of my experience as a deaf child in a mainstream (oral) school

I became deaf through meningitis a few months after my fourth birthday. Residual hearing allowed me to continue to hear sounds with the use of hearing aids. This was in 1966.

On recovery from my illness, I attended a local mainstream school, Soon after; I transferred to another mainstream school. within which was a Partially Hearing Unit (PHU). No sign language was used at this school. Some of the other children In the PHU would use sign language to one another, but only occasionally, thus we used to talk mainly.

When we had classes, we wore powerful radio aids. By the use of these and lip-reading I would be to follow what the teacher was saying in the classroom, but was a great struggle. However, in my final years at this school I was receiving some good grades and making friends, deaf and hearing.

My parents asked what secondary school I would like to go to on finishing at the PHU. I would have preferred to have gone to one of two schools, to be with other deaf children I had became friends with at the PHU, but I ended up at the local school, which, was totally mainstream.

I still recall my first day there, when I felt completely isolated and had no idea what was being said or going on around me. I went along with everything and was desperate not to stand out in any way.

This meant that I covered up my deafness as much as I could, and involved the strategy of pretending that I understood most of what was being said around me. I was eager not to be seen as deaf any way. I would often sit at the back of classes, making it difficult for me to follow lessons, so I had to copy things or try to catch up at a later stage with the teacher of the deaf who used to see me once a week.

The most destructive part of the process of going to a mainstream school was the total loss of any recognition I was a deaf person. This involved not only a distancing from other deaf children, but a phobia against anyone who was deaf. For example, three children in their final year at the school had been friends of mine at the PHU, and sometimes they would communicate in sign language. I avoided them at all costs, and the one time I remember us coming together I was aloof and wanted very little to do with them.

A second example, a teacher brought myself and my best deaf friend together one day, and I spent the whole time wanting the day to end since I felt so uncomfortable with him. A third example, on two occasions when I was with friends and a van full of deaf children drove by, I threw obscene gestures at them, much to the amazement of my friends.

The first two years were worst. l became a bully terrifying a boy who had become a close friend, to try to prove myself to my peers. I punched him in full view of the class and teacher. l had very few real friends. I relied on my younger (hearing) brother for friends, as we used to hang around in the evenings with a group near where we lived.

The real affects of my education in a mainstream setting, without any access to sign language or any sense of a positive deaf identity was evident when I finished my education.

To someone who wants to measure my ability to relate to people, to understand speech and to speak, and to have a level of intelligence that one would expect of a 17-year old, you would say my education had been a resounding success – for a deaf child anyway.

My speech was clear, I left school with three 0 levels (which was above what my parents and a lot of other children had managed), and had the distinction of winning a medal for cross country running and representing my school football team.

I had high hope of entering the banking or computing industry, but no-one wanted to employ a deaf adult who could not use the telephone. I applied for 60 jobs in all, receiving about 6 interviews, failing all, so to desperation accepted a post as a cleaner.

I lived at home with my parents and brother. I had no friends to call upon and would long for friends, not from the mainstream school, but from my junior school. This when I was 18. I would spend the weekends at home watching television, or I would go out on my own. Every time I would meet anyone, I would be completely lost for what to say. It took me a while to realise that this was because I could not understand what was being said, so could not contribute, and would avoid participating In groups. Those hearing people around me (at my place of work) thought I had social and psychological problems because of this, which took me completely by surprise.

The story from here to the present day (now in my mid-thirties) – that

Is for half of my life – has been one long struggle to come to terms with my communication needs. It is a struggle that has been totally unnecessary, and I am committed to ensuring others do not suffer in the way I have done.

I have had several 'nervous breakdowns'. I have suffered from depression, severe stress and anxiety (including panic attacks), and was diagnosed as having a neurotic disorder by a psychiatrist. I have seen several Counsellors, and continue to do so, and feel this Is all that help me keep going.

By recognising I was having problems, it gradually dawned upon me that I was getting nowhere by relying on other hearing people for friendships and romance, and denying my deaf identity. When l began visiting deaf clubs I felt so much more relaxed. One of the most surprising things I learnt was that my experiences were common – i.e., other deaf people went through the same process of mixing in hearing communities and having great difficulties – the difference with me seemed to be that I came to this point quite late.

In the deaf clubs communication barriers were not so difficult. Not only was I also deaf, but I began learning sign language, and I was able to be involved in groups, unlike at any other time in my life as an adult. I also began to make real lasting friendships.

I have been angry for a long lime that I was denied the opportunity to learn sign language from an early age, that I had to go through such negative experiences before realising my place was with deaf people , and I would prefer a form of sign language as a means of communication, and so not have to rely on speech and my residual hearing.

A bilingual approach would have been my preferred option. I could have learnt to read, speak and developed English after I had become deaf, but rather than relying on a struggle to lip-read, life could be far easier if I had been able to have a visual language. Then I believe I would have achieved far more than I had done at school. But just as importantly, I wanted to have remained alongside my deaf peers. I specifically asked for this when I was 12 but it did not happen.

I am now committed to ensuring that deaf children do not undergo the same experiences that I did. I am no expert on all the issues of education, but all I do know is that the bad experiences I went through, i.e. oral mainstreaming, was an abuse I am still trying to recover from.

Steve Emery
January 1998

INVISIBLE

No one listens,
She's only deaf -
Gave her a poor education
Now they can say she's half educated,
she doesn't understand,
so no need to ask
For her opinion.

She's not got any proper opinions.

Hot-headed
Paranoid
Mixed up.

But she sees with a seeing eye
Things hearing people can't hear
And she dreams
Wonderful dreams

Jill Jones
August 1994.

3   J's feelings

My feelings are mixed about my experience as a D/deaf person.

I was born with a very slight hearing loss, only my mother seemed to know. Doctors didn't believe her. When I started school along with my twin sister who had good hearing, my mother informed the teachers about my hearing loss and how best to deal with it. Each time I had a new teacher my mother would tell them a list, like sitting me at the front of the class so I could hear and lip-read better, not to have too much noise, etc. At this time in my life I didn't feel different to anyone else. As far as I can remember, there was a little disruption to my young life.

When I was older I had an illness that took most of my hearing. This left me feeling: why me? Why not my sister? Life didn't change, I just couldn't hear well. I had hearing aids fitted and at the age of 11 was sent to another school. Away from home. This was hard, not being part of a family, well, that's what I felt. At this school I found it easier to understand. I had Special Education lessons as they were called then (now called Special Schools.)

I could not feel part of family life, not hearing so good I lost a lot of the conversations that was going on around me. I started to feel left out, not able to fit in and make friends. I became a bit of a loner. Never going out much, not like my twin sister. She seemed to have more friends than me.

I did do exams and passed with average grades. On leaving school, it was when I tried to get involved with the Deaf community. This was hard. I was seen as an oral person, not a signer. Although my signing skills were good (if I say so myself) it didn't seem to help. It was when I was 22 years old and I had gone into nursing that I met other Deaf people. Oh, I had known about Deaf people before but only met a man who was Deaf but he was a son of my mum's friend. So that I felt didn't count.

Anyway I joined a new Women's' Group at the local Deaf club. Here I found a mixed group. Some Deaf from birth, some like me who had gone Deaf and others. To find people who felt like me was great, time to belong. My so-called quiet life had new meaning to me. I decided then to become more involved with the Deaf community.

I visited Deaf clubs, met Deaf people, but still no joy. I was seen as a J who can speak, not a J who was Deaf. I took signing classes to see if this helped. I could sign but thought this may help. No way. As the years went by I tried everything but nothing worked. I could not fully enjoy the world of the hearing as I could not hear well. Nor could I fully enjoy the world of the Deaf. Not being Deaf from birth, the Deaf Community just didn't want to know me.

The thing that opens a door into the Deaf World, for me, was when I was 26 years old. I got onto a youth workers course for Deaf people. I started a youth club at the local Deaf Centre. From this I join in with meetings and other things. The Deaf Community saw me as a person who could use my voice but also talk to the young Deaf people who used sign language as their first language. All my life I had been in the hearing environment (and still am most of the time) living, working, socialising, but now I could join in with the Deaf Community.

I am now 33 years old and I still have times when I don't fit into either world, but over the past 5 years I have found others like me who have found it hard to know where they belong. One thing I have learnt is to talk about how I felt and to become proud of who I am not what people think I should be. If we all share with each other then the them and us situation within the Deaf Community will go and all who have any type of hearing loss will be **D**eaf and not **d**eaf.

June Battye
1998.

4 *Working through the pain of change*

I wrote the following article from personal experience and following a conversation I had with Jill Jones. I wish therefore to make it clear that this has not arisen from research or from counselling sessions with clients I have held while employed as a counsellor or in training. Rather, this is a hypothesis, open for debate and questioning.

Jill and I have encountered people in our lives, read stories and experienced for ourselves what it means to go from being in a situation when you are living in a world surrounded totally by people who are not deaf, being totally unaware of your own identity, to being more congruent about who you are and the importance of deaf identity to your own self. This later point inevitably means being part of the Deaf community in some way, but the journey from the two points is one that can be littered with feelings of pain and hurt. Could it be possible to develop a 'stages theory' to identify this process, and highlight the stages the person is likely to undergo? I believe this to be possible.

In attempting to define these stages I wish to make a number of points clear. In the field of counselling and psychotherapy, Carl Rogers (1995 ed.) developed a similar stages theory. He did this as a result of years of counselling practice – there seemed to be a common process people went through as they undertook counselling. However, this I mean their general progression from being a person who is not aware of how their deafness is an important part of themselves, to be a general acceptance of themselves as a deaf person. It was also be a grave mistake to believe a person can effectively be 'pigeon-holed' into one of these stages – this should rather be seen as a fluid process.

The aim is two fold. Firstly, to highlight to deaf and hearing people ,ex-mainstreamers and non-mainstreamers, insight into the process ex-mainstreamers may be going through at any one time. This process can be extremely frustrating and painful, and involve a total transformation if an individual moves from one end of the spectrum to another. Secondly, Deaf and non-Deaf may benefit from being aware of these stages, so as best to enable them to understand and support the person, be it personally or professionally. As for *when* they are at a stage or *what* might trigger it, who knows? Each individual will be unique and will be the only person who knows how or why this may have come about.

With these preliminaries over, let me now turn to the stages. I identify four main ones, although it is probably more likely there will be 'sub-stages' a certain points in time. The first stage I will call the *statis* stage, or 'norm'; the second , a period of *self-conflict*, or struggle; the third, the *breakthrough* stage or 'revolution'; the fourth, I would call a period of *acceptance*.

So, to begin, the *statis* stage. At this stage, the ex-mainstreamer is, generally, unaware there is any difficulty at all. This can range from the person who has no concept at all of being deaf, to the person who does have some idea but does not consider themselves 'really deaf' or as part of the Deaf community, or of a group called 'deaf people'. None of this should be at all surprising, since the person will have experienced pressure from the dominant hearing society that they can 'be little different from a hearing person if they learn to speak, lip-read, etc' or that 'having a hearing aid is no different from having and wearing a pair of glasses'.

Other words that could possibly characterise this stage are: being in denial, a situation of pretence or 'falseness', but these are really inaccurate by themselves for the person does not feel in a state of denial or pretence. They feel perfectly real, and will wonder what all the fuss is about. They will feel relatively OK about themselves, and if there are problems it will not be considered something they can do much about.

Stage two is where the deaf person is in a state of *self-conflict*. They begin to recognise 'something is wrong'. It may well be that they feel this 'wrong' is related to a general difficulty or problem that they may or may not be experiencing – stress/anxiety, drink/drug/abuse, violence (either against themselves or others), a sense of low confidence and self esteem, etc. These may, in fact, be a smokescreen for a deeper crisis of identity , an unconscious conflict of being lost between two worlds.

However, slowly the individual is recognising that there is something about their identity which is troubling them, which they had not been aware of during stage one. They begin to understand, perhaps only vaguely, that they know little about themselves and their deafness. Jill Jones has referred to deaf people who identify with the hearing world as being 'think hearing', and this is how they are at stage one (J. Jones, 1996). During stage two, however, the person struggles to maintain a 'think hearing' status while at the same time trying to make sense of themselves as a deaf person. This is a struggle that can be along one, taking up a lot of energy and frustration.

It is perhaps more accurate to state that there are two parts to this stage two process. The first part, where there is only a vague idea of 'something wrong', and the second part where the person is aware there is 'something wrong' but a feeling there is very little that can be done, so the person soldiers on, carrying on the self-conflict to breaking point.

Stage three is the dramatic stage, that I call *breakthrough*. It can, however, seem more like 'breakdown' to the person who is in the throes of this experience. They know 'something must be done' and that they need to do it. Their life must change. They understand themselves as torn between two worlds – deaf and hearing. They know they are deaf, that there is an identity there, but it's difficult to come to terms with since for so long they are been 'think hearing'. The person may, in fact, veer totally towards identifying with BSL Deaf people, but find many of those in the community question whether they are 'really deaf'.

Changes they attempt to carry out with people around them will be likely to lead to conflict with others – noticeably parents and family, close friends and partners. Change will likely mean not only that they will take up and learn sign language, but that they will want others to learn too so communication can be easier all around. Family ties and relationship can be broken and new ones formed as a result.

Inevitably, this stage gives rise to the most powerful feelings and emotions. Some of these are likely to include grief, anger, depression and a sense of unreality. They will grieve for the lost opportunities, for the person they once were, struggling, isolated and unaware. They will be very angry that they were allowed by others to be left in this position. Most likely, it is parents/guardians who will experience the full force of this anger. There will be depression and loneliness as they attempt to come to terms with the change. There will be an air of surrealism about the changes as they view former circle of friends and others with new eyes and from a deaf perspective.

There is no going back, and this stage is unlikely to be undertaken without experiencing great pain and remorse. It could be reasonably split again into two separate sub-stages – the first where all the emotions come bursting forth in one great avalanche, and the second, which will be of less intensity but more drawn out. The stage, painful as it may be, is nevertheless healthy for the ex-mainstreamer.

Once these emotions are felt and experienced, there is a tendency to move towards the fourth stage, when the person is more *accepting* of themselves. This stage will most likely overlap with the previous one as there may be a general acceptance while feelings are worked through. The acceptance stage is reached when the person has negotiated their place in the Deaf community with ease – they may decide they are happy in both worlds to an equal extent, or perhaps with a little step in the Deaf community while continuing to mix mainly in the hearing world, or vice versa. In fact there are no general guidelines, especially if there are other factors involved, for example if they are also trying to overcome other abuses in their lives. The main characteristic of this stage is that the person has a more realistic outlook on how they communicate with others in both worlds, and have made changes and plans to live more resourcefully, as a deaf person.

Acceptance, however, does not mark an ending: it could in fact be said to be a new kind of status. One thing is certain – there is no going back to the original status and there will be no more self-conflict as it is known in stage two, although some characteristics of stage three might always be present (a sense of unreality for example).

Identifying this stages process I do not want to give the impression I believe all ex-mainstreamers go through this process. That would be erroneous, for each individual is unique. It is probably fairer to write that there will be characteristics of each stage at certain times in the process of development. For example, stages two and three might be relatively mild , with little sign of struggle, pain, loneliness or loss. It will depend on the individuals 'support network' – for example, if they have a Deaf partner or friends, or supportive, understanding and caring parents, as they become aware of their identity. It would appear, however, that the majority will experience a degree of pain.

I am aware that as I write the above I write of 'worlds' as if there are only two, but of course there are lots of different worlds and identities, and certainly I am not arguing it is this simple. The key point, however, is that the ex-mainstreamer may never have before considered themselves to be 'deaf' in any way, they may have no or little contact with other deaf people, so to become aware of their deafness is a kind of awakening. They will see the differences between themselves and those close to them, who are mainly going to be hearing people, and I would say it is an empowering process to think in terms of one world and another in this context. Once this happens, the deaf person will then find their own meanings and their own ways to describe their total world.

Whether a 'stages theory' can be argued or not, in these last few years of the millennium, 93-97% of deaf children attend mainstream schools, with none or little opportunity to explore deaf identity, culture or history. Jones (1996) In the quest to 'normalise' deaf children, there is likely to be lot anger about in our community. That can be channelled in many directions, including political protest, which would be a positive thing. It is when that anger turns inward that the ex-mainstreamer can feel a pain no human being deserves. The stages-theory can be one way of understanding the pain of change such a person is likely to go through in the search of self-awareness.

Steve Emery
Summer 1997
Revised July 1999

5 Lost Deaf People and their Needs PART I

Talk given at the Mental Health and Deafness
Conference in Birmingham 1996.

The Rights of Man and the Human Needs Theory

The Deaf Ex-Mainstreamers Group (DEX) was created some two and a half years ago, partly based on the human needs and conflict resolution theories, which we believe are valid for the whole of the deaf population. We aim to resolve the negative aspects of being deaf amongst mainstreamed deaf people and turn it into positive acceptance. Mainstreamed deaf people are subjected to the hearing populace's norms with resulting stressful lives, pretending to understand, pretending not to be deaf, pretending to themselves that they are hearing people – even thinking that they are hearing. The Deaf community reinforces these negative feelings by rejecting those who do not conform to their norms

This situation, of being lost between two worlds (not the best, but the worst of both), begins in childhood and lasts throughout life.

It begins when the deaf child feels lost in the playground and when classmates are socialising, through to not grasping what is going on, either fully or partially, so not feeling in control of the environment. This develops into a loss of confidence in ability to relate or to achieve, which then results in loss of self-esteem. It is a downward spiral which permeates the deaf child's life. We will look at the long-term effects of mainstreaming later.

Conflict within the Deaf Communities

There are many identity groups and consequent identities:

Hard of Hearing, partially-hearing or deaf, profoundly deaf, stone deaf, oral (hearing-focused or think-hearing), deaf, half-deaf, deafened, deaf and (the offensive word) dumb, born-deaf, or born-hearing, turned deaf, deaf with a small 'd' or a big 'D' and many more identities thus creating conflicts arising from the imposed set standards of behaviour and norms. The biggest thing existing, the definition of 'D' and 'd'. That is creating conflict and rejection, thus weakening the campaigning position within the deaf community whilst squabbling among ourselves, rather than creating a powerful stand to gain equal opportunities in society. Conflict also prevents deaf people from becoming culturally Deaf.

Conflict exists in all minority groups and where countries struggle for territory, created by divisions and imbalance of power. However, to retain their power, hearing people have only to allow this situation to continue, in the same way as imperialists do. Normalisation is the way to ensure that deaf people are maintained in a weakened state, for we can never become hearing people however hard we try.

Evidence from DEX

Since the inaugerisation of DEX we have publicised our aims through various means, via the media, workshops, seminars and conferences; we have made contact with deaf people regarding their experience of mainstream education and consequent mainstreamed adulthood. They have not been easy to find: lost in the hearing world and unaware of their need to be "found". Once aware, they are asking for a vast amount of support from us which we are not ready to provide. However, we can begin to compile evidence by building up data and statistics. Here is one of the letters:

> I read your article "Making the Transition to Deaf" and I cried. It has taken me a long time to teach myself to be Deaf and I am still sorting out the Deaf me.
>
> I am a Youth Project Development Worker. Many of my young people are struggling with their Deaf identity and within this area there is a very "oral/aural" policy, therefore many young people are afraid to voice their communication needs."

From this, and many other similar letters, indicates growing evidence of the behavioural problems emerging, of deaf children isolated, bulled and fearful in hearing schools, and also amongst deaf adults. Bristol University research found, in 1995, that 93.7% of deaf children now attend hearing schools. We can forecast what will happen to them when they leave school. This pattern of development will continue unchecked, unless positive steps are taken now to counteract the damage done by normalisation.

Government Cutbacks

Consecutive Governments have cut back on the cost of deaf schools; since the 1950's the integration policy has resulted in deaf schools being closed. Integration increased dramatically in the 1980's from 64% of deaf mainstreamed children to the 93.7% current day figure. The disability movement has recently put more pressure on the Government for children not to attend segregated schools, and the Education Acts of 1981, and the recent 1993 Education Act encourages parent partnership, where parents can make decisions about school placements.

Faced with out of area schooling or local education, parents naturally choose the latter. There is a consensus of opinion that it is in deaf children's best interests to be integrated.

However, despite this the DfEE. has begun to cut back on communication support. Statementing has changed to a complex system of stages before acquiring a statutory assessment. Parents wishing to amend their deaf child's placement or to change it have to play a Snakes and Ladders game with the education system. It is becoming a Catch 22 situation. If there is insufficient investment in mainstream education to meet even the basic needs of deaf children, there will be real costs to Social Services Departments and the N.H.S. in the future, as you can see from our evidence.

The issue of mainstreaming began with a trickle but has escalated in the last fifteen years and is beginning to be felt within the Social Services Deaf Teams fairly recently. Social Services Departments with respect to N.H.S. Community Care Act, 1992, have clear duties and responsibilities towards service users, but with limited fundings. Out of the blue there is now a trend – deaf adults are coming in to ask for help from Social Services who are mainstreamers from the 70's and 80's era. They are the lost deaf people who, after a lull of many years, suddenly surfaced. This trickle can become a waterfall within the next five to ten years. This is in combination with the Government's decision to make a 25% cutback to Social Services which could deny access to the provisions of either the Mental Health Section and/or Deaf Services.

Practitioner Liaison

Historically, there has always been poor liaison between local education authorities and Social Services Departments with respect to referrals of deaf children and their families. Unless the Social Worker with Deaf people has strong negotiating skills, or the Head of Service for

Hearing Impaired children understands the issues, it is often the case that the two agencies do not work together. It is imperative now that there is a written policy whereby practitioners compile a strategy to ensure that deaf children are acculturalised. Several areas are already doing this. We will look at some during the course of this joint paper.

Conclusion

Like others before us, we also challenge very ingrained assumptions, which, as Van Cleve (1993) says are:

> "First, that Deaf people must become as similar to hearing people as possible if they are to be happy or successful, and second, that a weak minority – in the case of Deaf people – must always adapt their culture to meet the cultural preference of the stronger majority."

Adam Walker

5 *Lost Deaf People and their Needs* PART II

Talk given at the Mental Health and Deafness
Conference in Birmingham 1996.

"How can you be yourself when you do not know who you are?"

This was said by a DEX member in response to my statement, "Be yourself, although you are the only deaf person in your hearing family".

It is not easy being yourself when you have been normalised. Every minute of every day, all of your life, from the cradle to the grave, society tells us all that we must conform to the norm. However, if you have learnt an identity, no matter how ill it fits, it is hard to undo it. Normalisation also does not give us scope for change; locked into the system it is hard to get out of it.

The majority of deaf mainstreamed children go on to marry or live with hearing partners. Most of us have no choice; we cannot sign so we do not meet Deaf partners, and even if we do, Deaf people would not necessary want to live with us; seen to have an attitude problem, "not really deaf" and not having Deaf values or norms there would be a cultural mismatch. As most ex-mainstreamed deaf people do not even meet other DEX people, having been educated apart from other deaf pupils, it is rare that they meet socially after school compared with the larger group of deaf people who marry or cohabit with hearing people.

I have thought long and carefully about how to write this paper. There are so many different kinds of relationships, each couple entering into the bond for so many different reasons that it could be generalising to try to discuss what happens in deaf/hearing partnerships. However, I have seen clear parallels from work and from DEX members' or deaf friends' relationships. There is an imbalance of power in deaf/hearing relationships which each couple has to address, in much the same way as women and men have to deal with. Deaf people who have not been taught how to behave as a deaf person are seriously endangered. If one does not know one's needs, it is hard, if not impossible, to be attracted to a person who knows how to meet the needs or to know how to ask the hearing partner to communicate effectively. Being mainstreamed individually, convinces the deaf person (and everyone around them) that they can cope by using residual hearing and lip reading. It may work in the short term, whilst the deaf person is still young with plenty of stamina.

As the couple gain more responsibilities, maybe bringing up a family, working and conducting their lives like hearing couples, then the cracks start to show. The deaf person needs communication support to survive; he or she does not know how to ask for it, because it has never been taught by other deaf people; this is Deaf acculturalisation. Normalisation will fail the deaf person as life makes more demands. Those few who do survive may have good support mechanisms in other ways, i.e. hearing partners or parents who become more responsive to the deaf person's needs and actually teach the deaf partner how to be more deaf. Where the hearing partner cannot make the adjustment, this further locks the deaf person in the relationship until it becomes intolerable.

Making the transition to being Deaf is almost impossible without support from one's family and friends. As John Donne states in his poem "No man is an island, entire unto itself". In "Bilingualism and Deaf Identity", Jones (1996) says that psychologists point out that collusive identities are based upon two or more people mutually creating each others' identities. When one changes, the other's identity has to change. The lover who ends the relationship leaves behind an ex-lover who does not want this new identity. The same for deaf people who begin to realise that they cannot function as quasi-hearing people as it is too tiring, or too boring sitting on one's own whilst the hearing partner is out or otherwise engaged, or that they feel they are being driven insane by feelings of being unloved and uncared for. This is simply because the hearing partner wants to have a "normal" relationship, thought that their deaf partner could manage with a hearing aid and/or lip-reading and all would be well. When the deaf partner begins to make the transition, this then shifts the power balance. Maybe there had been an element of "interpreting" in the relationship – explaining English, helping to pronounce words, giving meaning to life with general knowledge teaching – all in a "My Fair Lady" type relationship towards a continuation of normalising the deaf partner.

It is not surprising that hearing partner's feel threatened by a transition to deafness as this will mean a sea change in the relationship. If the hearing partner can make the transition towards Deaf culturalisation with the deaf person, then there is a chance the relationship can be safe. Learning sign language together, attending deaf events and clubs together, learning about Deaf culture at the same rate, being actively interested – only then can the relationship survive; unless they are both content to live separate lives, or unless the deaf person tolerates being a "think-hearing" person because the transition is too daunting.

Those deaf people who obtain status in the hearing world will very often be happy enough to be a "think-hearing" person. Normalisation will fit the bill because as any black person or woman knows, to climb the career structure, one has to be pseudo white or male. It is similar for disabled or deaf people. All minority group members have to work twice as hard to prove their worth in the career stakes. The reason why there are so few high flyers in industry who are congenitally and more than mildly deaf is because of the sheer pressures there are in communicating and competing on unequal terms in the workplace. If, added to this, there is no real empathy in the marriage or live-in relationship, then this is additional strain.

As I said earlier, normalisation leads to a collusive situation for deaf people brought up in mainstream schools. It is not in hearing partners' or hearing children's interests to change; why should they if everything seemed to be going well? The deaf partner/mother/or father may have appeared to cope, the family have got used to the dynamics and that was how it was. When the deaf person starts to make demands such as, "please speak more slowly", or to turn their hearing aid off for a rest, then that is seen to be selfish, nagging or being unreasonable. The family may have been proud of the deaf member's attempts to be a hearing person – "she talks so well", or "he never mentions his deafness". Referring to being deaf is seen to be self-pitying, not noble or brave, and a sign of weakness. Non-disabled people regard us as martyrs and saints. By breaking that taboo we are sharply brought into line.

The deaf person ends up in a no-win situation – if we try to be hearing, we could continue to feel uncared for life. If we try to become deaf we may lose our loved ones. Whatever we do we are doomed to fail.

The deaf person has no choice but to give in or to be seen as a rebel. Alice Walker (1992) says: "Because of this (oppression), I must defy you, the outsider; even though it may be wrong, to be what is left of myself."

"To be what is left of myself..." the last remnants of the deaf self that lies dormant after years of normalisation. The lost self. The lost deaf person in the hearing family, in the workplace and in the community. Even more frightening is losing the other identities of mother/father, wife/husband/lover, child or older parents, whilst seeking one's own selfhood, which is crucial for development. Weissel (1988) states that hearing groups can have a derogatory attitude leading to "deindividu-ation and depersonalisation". Depersonalisation strips one's ego so that one feels unreal and odd and that there is no reality. There is no purpose or base to work from. That is madness. That is the stark, bleak knowledge that there is nothing left: all is lost. Identity is crucial to our personality development. To strip away our deafness is crude debase-ment of our essential personality.

If we are made to think we are hearing people then we try to act this way; in this "think-hearing identity" we are engaging in a dance with our hearing families who want us to delude ourselves, as well as them-selves being deluded. What does this tell us? That we are not being loved for ourselves as Deaf people, therefore we are essentially bad because we are not good enough "hearing people". Susie Orbach (1996) Psychoanalyst, states "a core infected with a sense of its own badness...feelings of badness , of wrongness, of not being fundamen-tally all right. Whatever (she) creates of value can become valueless in the face of her core feelings of badness". This void, she says, can be filled with too much compulsive work, giving, sex, food, drugs or socialising. However much one does, though, it never appeases the feeling of being a loser, "dispersing of self".Orbach (1996)

Vic Finkelstein (1989) says: "This is yet another contradiction: the emphasis is on making disabled people normal, the result is you feel even more abnormal, more disabled."

Normalisation can be cruelty far worse than sexual or physical abuse for it can last a lifetime. It can make for deeply unhappy people, as DEX is discovering. In a small study of "Actual and Perceived Attitudes to Deafness" Furnham and Lane,(1984)deaf subjects were found to have very negative attitudes towards their social life and inte-gration with hearing people. All the deaf subjects had extensive contact with hearing people. It indicated the low self-esteem that is prevalent amongst deaf people. Russian regimes convinced dissenters that they were wrong to question the state and they became mad. Do deaf people, in order to find their Deaf selves, have to undergo this pain, and their families to suffer with them? Do we have to go through life trying to instil self-confidence, self-pride and self-love in ourselves? DEX has, (as Adam Walker has just explained in Chapter 5 Part I), discovered a common pattern and reasons amongst deaf ex-mainstreamers and ex-deaf oral school pupils for our behaviour.

"The whole process of development can be seen as an attempt to discover one's own identity; and since this cannot be done in isolation, the development of a person is conditioned by his relationship with other persons in all its extent.", Anthony Storr(1964).

There is much research done in the field of identity development. It informs us that similarly, a deaf child taught in isolation in a hearing school without a deaf peer group or role models is lost. Personal identity is shaped by group and social identity. Each mainstreamed deaf child will become a lost adult, not fitting in the hearing world and unable to relate to signing deaf peers. No-one ever remarks how inhumane it is that deaf people, in the main, cannot communicate effectively with each other. I, for one, find it extremely difficult to understand many deaf mainstreamed children and young people who are severely or profoundly deaf and who cannot sign. It is hard to work with them because of this.

Those deaf children who attended mainstream schools with others in units have a better fighting chance as will those who attended oral deaf schools. At least they belonged to a mini-deaf community and had a group identity with which to shape their own understanding of themselves and their needs. They are in a better position to make deaf friends and, therefore, to learn to make relationships and probably to fall in love and live with deaf partners. If they do marry or have live-in relationships with hearing people they will be more likely to know how to ask for their communication needs to be met from the start and set the precedent, i.e. the hearing partner will perhaps learn to sign.

As they are more likely to be profoundly deaf, the hearing partner will be clearer about needs, whereas moderately or severely deaf people can look more like hearing people.

This only proves how important it is that deaf education is not based on normalisation. Speaking for choices? Certainly not signing for choices! The educationalists' argument that being brought up orally/aurally leads to more choices in adult life is out of date and totally untrue. It may have provided us with better access to a broader curriculum in the days when deaf schools were unable to teach a wide range of subjects but deaf schools are improving. It may have enabled "partially hearing" children to "cope" alongside hearing children and to learn how to behave in the hearing world, and, therefore, to access the professions, as I did. Hearing socialisation is a prerequisite for all deaf children for that very reason.

It should, however, *never* be at the expense of the acquisition of a healthy, positive Deaf self or identity. To achieve that there has to be Deaf enculturalisation for all deaf children as well. The two "isations" go hand in hand. Only then can deaf children have a real choice when they become adults; and that choice will be to be confident, positive Deaf people who are part of Deaf culture, can play their part in hearing society. To have choice there has to be two options.

Deaf Acculturalisation

There are a great many obstacles to the setting up of Deaf acculturalisation schemes. It would seem obvious that Social Services Departments are the vehicles for change, given recent legislation; the Children Act 1989 which encourages deaf children to register as "children in need" and where provision must be made for advice, guidance and counselling of families of deaf children. The deaf child's needs must be taken into account when planning service provision. These are within the terms of the Act.

The N.H.S. and Community Care Act, 1992 stipulates that service users must play an active role in service provision. Deaf consumers of the education system and particularly DEX members, should be actively involved in supporting parents in the understanding of Deaf culture in its widest sense and in strategic planning with Education Departments. The Education Act, 1993 Code of Practice has as its fundamental principle that "the needs of all pupils who may have special educational needs either throughout or anytime during their school careers must be addressed". It also states that "the needs of most pupils will be met in the mainstream." The Education Section of The Disability Discrimination Act 1995 is based on the recent educational legislation and supports mainstream education. This must be challenged with respect to deaf children. Deaf children who attend mainstream schools need alternative provision within hearing schools to current practice; models of good practice must be researched and L.E.A.'s be prepared to change. Deaf people are debating the problems mainstreaming has caused in the Deaf community and the B.D.A. Education policy, although in my view still not forward thinking enough, advocates a model school.

However, other Deaf people have been "articulate critics of the co-education of deaf and hearing children". George Wing and Elizabeth Fitzgerald were partially Deaf people who found "academic integration a humiliating and destructive experience". This was 1906. DEX is not saying anything new about the school experience. A hearing Wisconsin Superintendent at that time, said "I suggest that the educated deaf, themselves, are more familiar with what is best for them and their kind than are the educated hearing".Van Cleve (1993).

Also in USA was a small integrated bilingual school run by Bartlett, which pioneered revolutionary ideas. He encouraged his deaf pupils to be joined by hearing siblings. Van Cleve(1993).

A mainstream infant school in Derbyshire currently has a bilingual approach where all the children, both hearing and deaf, are exposed to sign language and are learning it naturally. A study of families with

31

deaf children in the 60s and again in 1991. Gregory(1991), came to the conclusion that "by far the most important predictive factor for the young deaf adults is not their education but their family background. Educational policies to be properly implemented, must have the understanding and support of parents".

This is Deaf acculturalisation in the hearing family – where everyone is comfortable about deafness, where it is seen as an asset, where a new culture can contribute to the development of each individual family member, bringing with it more tolerance, understanding and respect for difference. The respect for difference model of integration is the equal opportunities model of integration that the normalisation model of integration is not, Van Cleve (1993). Normalisation is all around us; there can be no escape from it. There is no need to be afraid that deaf children will become ghettoised if alternative language and cultures are introduced to the family and educational setting. Children assimilate different social models more easily than adults and will become bicultural or tricultural. Social Services Departments have a crucial role to play in this Deaf/hearing socialisation process, not only to liaise effectively with other agencies in explaining the needs of deaf people to be bicultural but also to play an active role in setting up a socialisation programme.

The Deaf/hearing acculturalisation programme aims to teach respect for differences. Without full respect there is no real love. If children are not respected they do not feel loved and thus cannot love or respect themselves. They cannot, therefore, achieve their full potential.

In expecting deaf children to conform to the norm we condemn them to a lifetime of self disrespect. If we truly have deaf children's interests at heart we must accept their different need for communication for them to be proud of having a different language and culture. Otherwise we can never, ever, be ourselves for we do not know who we are.

Jill Jones

6 *I did not know what education was for*

I was diagnosed by doctors at 18 months of age, as being deaf. I became deaf through rubella. My mother knew I was deaf from early age, and my father was concerned, he tried to be supportive, although he was working full time. This was in 1960s. 'Where boom jobs were full.'

When diagnosed as deaf, the professionals told my parents to practise using lipreading and oral methods, I think signing was banned then. My parents could never understand what I was saying, I was very patient and tried not to get too frustrated. I remembered just following my parents, brother and two sisters wherever they went. I never knew where I was going until I got there. My youngest sister became my interpreter.

My parents remembered I started to speak about 8 years old, my parents never had experience of deaf family, and I was the only deaf person in the family. My parents are churchgoers and they used to pray for me to speak. During that time, I talked more than ever. Then my parents are praying for me to shut up! Because I would speak to anyone I could understand and lip read easily.

I do have some hearing with my hearing aid, without it I am deaf, one of my ears is deaf (cannot even use powerful hearing aid). The other ear can hear with hearing aid on. By that I can hear sound around me, not far away. I can hear radio talk, but only hear the mumbles. I repeatedly record the sound of music, I maybe get to know the first line and the rest is mumbled. I can hear people's voices around me with hearing aid on, I do not mean I can hear what they say. I rely on lipreading and voice at the same time, even without hearing aid, I still understand by lipreading,

My earliest memory about the hearing aids; I used to switch off at times. On one occasion I went to the garage, I saw some paint on the shelves. I saw a step to it and stepped up and managed to prise open the paint tin and then poured it over my parent's car and came back to the house. I was happy.

My father looked at me then looked at the garage. Off he went to look in the garage. He came back, fuming out and really had a good go at me. Then I switched my hearing aids off, looking at my father's face going red. My mother saw me switching them off, she burst out laughing at me. Now my father saw the funny side of this story and said nothing. I switched off my hearing aids because it was not nice to lipread. It really was a learning period.

At the age of eight, I remember, practicing for ages, learning better and better words and how to pronounce them correctly. I have never forgotten the letter "P". It took me hour after hour to get it right at school. With the candle in front of me, I was really fed up with it, so I kept blowing it out. The teacher got very cross with me, I remember she told me off (though I'm still in contact with her).

At school, there was loads of misunderstanding. I always looked into books and worked it out from there or looked at the blackboard a few times. I went to my PHU (Spin Gate School) at an early age the coach came to pick me up and dropped me off after school with other deaf children. I believe there were eleven of us. I did have afternoon sleeps in the school; they had beds laid out for all of us. I do know we had a picture book (home to school book) to take home for my parent to write about what happened at weekends.

I was late starting to learn to write, I was late in learning to say "mother" or mum or father or dad. When I was little I used to call them by their own names! We went on holiday every year, but I never knew where I was going for a weekend away. I was the one following like a rabbit; I've always played with my brother or sisters but did not have friends. The reason was that they lived a long way away. When I was at school in lessons, I always sat with hearing people but at break time, I always mixed with other Deaf people. We used some gestures and lipreading and play by acting.

I think when I was about six years old my father learned to sign, I began to understand my father as it had been hard to lipread what he was saying. My mother was easy to lipread. My sister took over as interpreter always telling my parents what I was saying. When I was eleven years old, I was not told that I was going to a new school. I just remember that there were long hot sunny days in 1976 and that I had a new uniform, which was posh, made me feel good, and a cap on my head, I felt well dressed! Soon the new school started, but it was just the same as the last school, hard to follow, and it was easy to feel mixed up. It took me a long time to settle down. They had a new PHU and I was one of the first deaf pupils to use it. There was special equipment in the unit, signing not allowed, and all communication in lipreading only. Mrs Preston was my first teacher – she was good and she did try to involve me. I was with her every lesson except English which I went to the PHU for. At break I always played with hearing friends not the deaf friends! My hearing friends always faced me to let me understand.

At class, a teacher always faced the blackboard to write. I always wrote things down but never understood the meaning of it. I did not know the right or wrong things to ask the teacher. My reading had improved but my English was going downhill, yet maths steadily improved. My education was very poor, I had to read and find out by copying from a friend. English I found out was an important subject to have when I was 18. I did not know what education was for, what it meant for future work. Finally at college I gleaned some understanding when I gained grade 3 for maths, grade 4 for English and 0-level Art grade B. English was the most difficult subject to understand – vowels in grammar and so on: these I did not comprehend till later.

In my school year, having hearing friends and knowing what was happening around me was interesting, but my education was very poor. At about the age of 12-13 we were given headphones in the PHU. When Teachers spoke, I didn't hear through the headphones, so every time the teacher asked me if I had got it on, I said "yes", I just put my headphone on to leave it switched off and lipread. Every time I went to the PHU I remembered I always helped other deaf pupils as best I could with their work. I got little work done for myself, as I missed out a lot by going to the PHU often, and never understood the course work because of lack of communication with the teacher.

I left school with few qualifications, my father got me a job, but I never knew what the job was. I got a job at British Leyland, where there was a deaf person who I knew from early school days. It was a small world. I went to college for a car mechanic's course to get the grades, but I never understood the teacher, I tried to copy other student's notes but could not understand them. When I took the exam, I failed. My sister helped me by asking her boyfriend (my future brother-in-law) who had done the same course, to give me advice. With the help of his easy-to-follow notes, within two weeks I revised the work, resat the exam and passed.

When I was 14, I went to a deaf youth club, not many deaf people there, but I did go a few times to chat and drink. Nothing much going on there. My elder sister dragged me to venture scouts, I had a good experience learning about camping and all sorts of other things. The only thing that I could not cope with was the leaders talking around the campfire at night, I just could not understand what they were saying. I went to bed early to avoid any talking. With the scouts I achieved the Duke of Edinburgh Award and the Queen's Scout Award. At 22 years old I was asked to become a leader for the group, I would have loved to, but turned it down due to communication difficulties. My sister was willing to help me but it was not fair to drag her around with me.

I became involved in FYD through a contact, which was brilliant and stayed with them for a number of years, organising camping weekends. It was hard work but rewarding working with deaf and hearing youngsters.

I also started an arts degree course at the age of 24 at Coventry University which I found hard work. It was very difficult without any interpreter, just lipreading and it was hell. I was trying hard to keep it up but still missed out a lot of information from the lecturer. Often I did not know what the meeting was about, as the lecturer always talked while you worked. I know the talking was not important all the time but I missed the essential information. My friends forget about my deafness just because I speak very well and think I am a normal person. I failed the degree as I did the wrong thing for three months in the last year of my course. There were new funds for an interpreter in the late 1990s. That's how I found out about my course work which was not right. The teacher had known about the situation, and when I challenged this in a long letter, it was agreed to allow me to retake the last year, but my confidence was shaken. It was very good experience and hard work, but lots of misunderstanding

At my workplace I have done the same work for 22 years, I have never liked the job but with my family needs, I need to earn a living . I use sign as well as speech, and at my workplace half don't understand and some do. A friend of mine told me about teletext television around 1990 as I never bothered with television before then. I watch more subtitled programmes, I cannot live without it or I can live without television, either way.

Looking back over the years I would love to go back in time and put some correct understanding of deafness and needs into schools. Schools can improve by providing good experiences and understanding of Deafness. All deaf people are different, but need deaf identity and culture as a base.

Ian Randell
2003

Brought up in a family where everyone can hear

Brought up in a family where everyone could hear
Hearing was "normal" that was made clear
Listen, try harder – you'll learn to speak well
Disguise the deafness, so no-one can tell.
Some think you're stupid, some think you're shy
But you can't be yourself, and you don't understand why
You feel that you're different, so you must take the blame
Try hard to conform, it will make you the same.

"You don't need deaf friends – you communicate fine –
Mix with hearing people you don't need to sign..."
I accepted this attitude, I'd known it so long
Then I opened my eyes and saw they were wrong
It was almost impossible trying to explain
My inner most feelings, I was causing them pain.
Why is it so hard to tell the people who care
Their ambitions and plans you just cannot share,
With a heart full of conflicting emotion -
I'd let them down by splitting my devotion:
They're in another world, they'd never really understand
I wanted something different in the future I had planned.

Keep fighting, keep searching, 'till you find the right shelf
Then relax and enjoy life – just being yourself!!!...

Kate Wheat
1995

7   *The Things I Remember*

My Education Before Work

One of my earliest memories is of falling asleep in nursery class through boredom and being sent home. When you can't hear you do tend to wander off in your mind. I think the early years were a bit 'vague' and I didn't connect to what was going on much. Family life at home was good. My parents and my brother were always there for me. So although I was socially isolated at school, I enjoyed being with my brother and felt supported by my family.

I had a hearing aid by the time I went to school and became aware of the difference between me and the other children. The headmaster called me 'Deaffy' in class and used to say that my hearing aid might as well be a matchbox with a piece of string and a cork in my ear. He didn't believe I was deaf when I started at his school and my parents had to get an educational psychologist to visit and inform him that I did have a severe high frequency loss of sound. In the fifties the hearing aid was a large body worn unit with two enormous batteries, one in each pocket of my shorts, which made them slowly sink down over my waist!

My performance was not good. I did best in Geography where there was a weekly test of countries which I rote learnt from the text and was always in the top three. Latin was another subject where what was missed in class could be learnt from a book. You just knew you wouldn't hear the majority of what was taught in class and you didn't expect to. I was very anxious as a child and I find it difficult to decide how much this was due to my disability, poor functioning and isolation, and how much my childhood personality.

I was sent to a public boarding school where my father had been as a child and two years later my brother joined me. I had a poor first year, after which it was decided to give me two hearing aids. After all I had a similar loss in both ears! For me that was when I started to catch up. I was still unable to hear a lot of what was said in class, in the house room and in the dormitory. This made me insecure, and I was lacking in social skills and confidence to a large degree. I enjoyed most parts of the school life including the sports and the scouts. It was a 'survival of the fittest' culture and within that I had to develop my own way of surviving as the only deaf child in a residential school of 450 boys.

My main interest was in science especially biology. I struggled with foreign languages, managing French, but being unable to hear the difference between the German vowels I was advised to leave those classes. Every child had to audition for the choir, and after my attempt to follow the scale without being able to hear the different notes beyond a certain level, the organist declared that I was not cut out for this. Sadly as that was the only criterion, that was the beginning and end of my musical education at school.

I went to university and found it very difficult to hear in the large lecture halls and in the laboratories. It was always a great struggle to take notes of the lectures and understand what was being said at the same time. I never received any assistance from the university with these difficulties and assumed it had to be like this. My time there was very intellectually stimulating and I really enjoyed it despite the difficulties. Social relationships started to become easier. Somehow I didn't meet any other deaf students and so had no way of validating my identity. I developed more ways of surviving in the hearing world.

My Working Life

I started working with children in 1970 with a local authority Children's Department and have remained doing this with Social Services as a social worker and team manager until recently when I started working in a children's planning team. My education in a mainstream school and at university was a poor preparation for working life. As a result of my experiences my confidence was low, my social skills were poor and I hated using the telephone.

At my first interview I was required to attend a medical on account of my disability. The doctor insisted on using the 'watch' test despite my informing him that I was unable to hear a watch ticking. As a result I was recorded as being deaf which did not really help to measure the hearing loss I had and was my first experience of how my disability was perceived in the employment field. When I started work I received no advice, guidance or help from my employer in relation to coping with my hearing loss in my work. My earlier childhood experience of being isolated when outside of my family and home, and of being excluded from social interaction, was repeated in aspects of my working life. This reinforced my strategies of avoidance of groups and situations where hearing and communication were stressful.

My first job was in residential work looking after boys in an approved school (at that time undergoing the change to community home school). It was an intense emotionally charged community working with eighty children many of whom had had damaging experiences at home and therefore showed behavioural problems. My house unit of twenty children all in one room produced a high level of background noise which made hearing difficult. Good communication was of course essential, and I struggled to make relationships and play a formative part in the life of the school. The best opportunities came with one to one conversations outside of the unit and with small group outings. One of my duties was driving a minibus over long distances to take children for weekend visits home, which I enjoyed, but it was difficult to hold conversations because of the noise and lack of face to face contact.

The next move was as a trainee social worker which gave good opportunities for one to one contact and working with people in their own home. It was also my first experience of working in an office and regular telephone use. At that time both my employer and I were unaware of telephone loop systems and I received no advice. I went through a very unsatisfactory time when I dreaded a telephone call. During my social work training at university I had five different placements and each time went through the same process becoming adept at avoidance.

When I started work as a qualified social worker I was placed in a large open plan office with two teams. By the end of my first week I knew I could not survive because of the noise levels. One of the managers immediately agreed to give up his office and so I coped. Some time later I acquired a telephone with an inductive coupler, a volume control and a second handset (wonderful!) and I started to become less anxious. Subsequently the teams moved to an even larger open plan office with only one room. Again I knew I would not manage so it was agreed I would move into the broom cupboard. This was a small room with no windows and a strip light which suited me because I wanted to stay in the team and I would have had to leave otherwise. I remained in that room for thirteen years.

During my time as a social worker and later as a manager I very gradually became more confident both as a person and as a worker. My telephone skills became much better. Hearing aids became more sophisticated. More professional advice and support became available. I received help, support and encouragement from colleagues, friends and family. I found I was less tense and able to relax more. This was in the context of local authority social work mainly with child protection and children in care which is stressful work. A recent survey in my local authority has established that the team manager's post for children is the most stressful job in the whole Council. I have worked in that job for twenty three years.

In that role I had to chair meetings, make decisions and record the meeting without any assistance. This is very difficult to do when you have to lip, face and body read several people, some of whom may be upset and angry, observe the dynamics and the undercurrents and manage the meeting. Taking notes at the same time detracts from your role as chair and reduces your ability to enable participation by members of the meeting. Needless to say it was exhausting work. As manager of the team I would have formal supervision with social workers and give them my full attention in discussing cases and supporting them in carrying out their work. I needed to lip read and concentrate all the time in order to supervise effectively. I found I could not do this and keep a legible record of the session at the same time, and it was not possible to remember everything afterwards.

I have given evidence in court on numerous occasions over the last thirty years. This was always a difficult arena to hear in, and more recently as my hearing has deteriorated slightly, I have been unable to hear and there has been no loop provided despite requests on several occasions. I had to fight the usual disability barrier with a large organisation displaying a big equal access at the front of the building and no working loops at all. On a number of occasions I was assured that there was now a working system only to find minutes before the court sat that this was not so. As a result of my complaints over two years supported by my management, there is now one of the twenty plus courtrooms in one of Leeds Courts fitted with a new working loop and more to follow (hopefully). What chance for non professionals in court?

Discrimination in my work has been noticeable in the area of promotion. Interviews are always difficult for hearing impaired people and I have found it very difficult to give a positive account of myself and my work in the standard intense thirty/forty minute interview. I did best in a two day exercise where I could demonstrate my abilities better, but this method of recruitment is rarely used. It is particularly disadvantaging for disabled people that track records are not used to inform interviewing panels about candidates. I have felt that I have hit the glass ceiling on occasions and attempts to overcome this have not been recognised by my employer despite the language of equality disseminating over the years into employment policy.

Life in the hearing world as hearing impaired person is a constant struggle to maximise your chances of hearing/ interpreting the majority of what is said/ communicated. In work life you continue not to hear the asides or the jokes, and social interaction can remain the isolating experience of your personal world. The strain of continually concentrating on trying to hear/interpret what is happening takes its toll. This 'always calculate state' (See Chapter 1 Making the Transition to Deafness) is something that has no end in sight. I have experienced it as a 'treadmill where one is competing to understand and keep up.' And this means you have to work harder and longer than your non disabled colleagues to achieve the same results. Colleagues in my team and in the management team were aware of my disability and supported me when they could Importantly, I was regarded and accepted as a colleague, team member and friend as equally as everyone else.

I joined a group for deaf and hearing impaired staff when it was formed several years ago, and then later joined DEX after hearing Jill Jones talk to us. These groups have been very helpful for me in moving to a more comfortable identity as a deaf person. This has contributed to a better approach to the hearing world at work.

Recently I have acquired a Conversor (a remote radio controlled microphone) which for me acts as a third ear, and it has been very useful at work in meetings. I have very much enjoyed, and am enjoying my work for Social Services, particularly the direct contact with clients and the team work with colleagues.

Brian Daltry
2003.

8 Bilingualism and Deaf Identity

Paper given at Mental Health and Deafness
Conference, 1994

Grosjean, (1984) amongst many other linguists, says that by virtue of knowing a language this confers upon one membership of a linguistic community. David Crystal (2000) also suggests that "switching to a minority language is very common as a means of expressing solidarity with a social group. The language change signals to the listener that a speaker is from a certain background; if the listener responds with a similar switch, a degree of rapport is established".

What is bilingualism? – "the obvious answer is", as David Crystal (1987) again says is "someone who speaks two languages". This is too complex an area to analyse today; briefly, if a person learns two languages at the same time – this is simultaneous bilingualism. If one language is learnt after the first (L1) then this is successive bilingualism. A person can have a dominant (or preferred) language or be sublingual in 2 languages. One can be a balanced bilingual whose fluency is equal in both languages. Dormant languages are those which are not used for a while.

Deaf people who are bilingual in the use of BSL and English indicate quite a range of bilingual variations. For the most part English will be the first language to which they were exposed, but many profoundly Deaf people take BSL as their dominant (or preferred) language.

In the case of deaf children, as with many other members of minority groups, the expectation is that they will learn the host spoken language of their country, so that they are monolingual, though many are sublingual. This is the maximum exposure hypothesis, which is exposure to the majority language even though children may find this exposure difficult (language bath – or drowning, as some linguists say).

Studies in status and inter group power relations with respect to language are extensive. All point to: "the vehement resistance to the bilingual programs is that the incorporation of minority languages and cultures into the school program confers status and power (jobs for example) on the minority group". This was said by Fishman (1977) et al whilst Cummins (1986) looked at how to empower minority group members but noted the disempowering constraints.

In 1981, the Swedish Parliament passed a bill (Prop 1980, 81:100) "that in order to function in society and amongst themselves deaf people must be bilingual". The Bill also acknowledged Swedish Sign Language as L1 and Swedish (spoken language) as L2.

If deaf people are to be able to relate to all other deaf people then competency is required in two languages with the ability to switch codes and/or languages. The contact language between the two languages are the pidgin forms Signed English or Signed Supported English. Paul Higgins (1990) points out how deaf people who speak and sign are more comfortable with others who also use their voices when signing . Carol Padden and Tom Humphries (1988) indicate that deaf people view deaf people not only in accordance with how they communicate but also by how they behave. A hard of hearing person who uses appropriate behaviour in the Deaf Community is seen as "Deaf but really hard of hearing". This is praise indeed for a partially deaf person. In UK the highest praise for someone who is not profoundly deaf is "looks like grassroots Deaf" or "one of us". In America, as in UK, "oral" is seen as a derogatory term "Hearing focus" or "Think-hearing" are those who come from well-off families who usually prefer their deaf child to be monolingual and "always plan" are those oral deaf people who have to "be alert to every possible situation in order to pass successfully" in the hearing world. Padden and Humphries (1988) I mention these different groups of deaf people to give a sample of the diversity of deaf identities and views about other deaf people within our community.

Why deaf identity?

Paul Higgins (1990) has this to say about being a member of a Deaf community – "members seldom face the difficulties and frustrations which arise when they navigate through the hearing world. A sense of belonging and wholeness is achieved which is not found among the hearing".

There is much research into identity. A brief dash into philosophy, sociology and psychology in the 60s and 70s, when identity came into being is summed up in the statement "the positive desire to identify oneself as a member of a group and a feeling of pleasure when one does so", Rose & Rose (1965). Jean Paul Sartre asks: "Who is a Jew? – a Jew is one whom other men consider a Jew".

Dashefsky (1976) says: "An Ethnic Group may be defined as a group of individuals 'with shared sense of people hood', based on presumed shared sociocultural experiences and/or similar physical characteristics. Such group may be viewed by their members and for outsiders as religions, racial, national linguistic and/or geographical. Thus, what ethnic group members have in common is their ethnicity, 'or sense of people hood', which represents part of their collective experience".

The Deaf Community has many ethnoid features but does not have natural parental guides to a heritage of traditions that are normally passed down within minority groups, except for some of the 10% of deaf children born to Deaf parents.

However, Fishman (1977) says: "ethnic groups in particular circumstances may all develop ethnoid attributes and self concepts, and given sufficient polarisation, some of them may attain the status of a full and distinct ethnicity". He goes on to say that it is "the pan-Western tendency" to always confer minority status on to ethnic groups.

So how can deaf children acquire their identities as deaf children? R. D. Laing (1969) says: 'The 'family romance' is a dream of changing others who define the self, so that *the identity of the self can be self defined*, by a re-definition of others". He was speaking of parents who attempt to mould their children into reflections of themselves, whereas children and young people are attempting to create their own identities. This occurs in most hearing families where there is a deaf child where a hearing, or quasi-hearing status is conferred on the deaf child, because parents naturally want their child to inherit the same value systems and behaviour patterns as themselves.

Deaf children may try to tear out from themselves this "alien identity" that they have been endowed with or condemned to, and create by their own actions an identity for themselves which they try to force others to confirm. However, most deaf children do not have access to an alternative identity on which to model themselves. One's first social identity is conferred on one. "We learn to be whom we are told we are" says Laing (1969)

Mainstreamed and deafened children may start to show a real interest in other deaf people ("the desire for an identity in the eyes of others" – Sartre (2001) and yet cannot break away from the ties of being the hearing child that their parents want them to be. This double-bind hypothesis (according to Laing) can also be collusive identity, in that there is a mutual evasion of truth and self-fulfilment. The family group bonds are stronger than the non-accessible Deaf community bonds. However, later many Deaf adults say that Deaf people are their family.

Sartre, amongst others, says it is a basic human need. Everyone needs to have complementary identities, i.e. to be a mother one must have a child, to be a husband one must have a wife, to be dominated one must have a dominator (Andrew Collier (1977) of Laing's theory). There are a large number of roles which people find themselves in or in terms of which they define themselves, and which depend for their existence on another person. This is crucial to one's self-conception, one's image of "who one is" or "one's being-for-others" Laing (1969).

Intense frustration arises from failure to find that other required to establish a satisfactory identity.

Depersonalisation

I am aware that there are those here today who question the validity of the need to have a Deaf identity, despite all the empirical evidence to the contrary. By so doing, there is the danger of depersonalising deaf people. If we are not hearing people (because we are not) then what have we to replace "think-hearing identity" with if we are not allowed to be Deaf? We are depersonalised in our homes, in our schools, in our workplaces. It can lead to mental illness; Webster (1985) says that depersonalisation is a "psycho-pathological syndrome characterised by loss of identity and feelings of unreality and strangeness about one's behaviour".

Deaf children's behaviour is also not seen to belong to them; it is rare that they are told that their behavioural aspects are prerequisite to being deaf. For example, with our more frequent use of eye contact deaf children are reprimanded and told not to stare. There are many examples of cross-cultural behaviours within hearing families where there is a deaf child which go unrecognised. Deaf children and young people often make their own "anti-script" (Eric Berne et al, 1987) but this turning around of their script still does not make them deaf. In other words, temper tantrums are seen as typical deaf child behaviour but this could not only be frustration due to communication break-down, but also because the child is reacting to the "hearing script" that the parent is endowing on him or her.

To prevent depersonalisation and identity loss or erosion, then identity development is central to each child's mental and physical health. Crystal (2000) suggests that there are five reasons for main-taining language diversity, one of which is "languages express diversity". He states that "language is an index, symbol and marker of identity," as presented by Colin Baker (2001), and that security and status as part of a shared existence is an essential marker of identity development.

Lynch (1992) states that historically, identity development was via (1) the family group or tribe (2) city state and single state nationalism (3) global rights and responsibilities and internationalism. He argues that we now recognise three major levels of group affiliation: local community membership (familial, ethnic, community) or other social local groupings not necessary linked to being in the same geographic place at the same time and national and international membership. Such group identities shapes our individual identity.

Culture Fatigue and Shock

How can the deaf child redefine their identities as not-really deaf people? When, as young adults, they attempt to become part of their Deaf community there can be rejection of one kind or another by Deaf members. Culture fatigue has been categorised as:

1) Cultural differences – the function of the differences between the foreigner's (or outsiders') culture of origin and the receiving society.
2) Individual differences – the ability of people to cope with new environments with demographic and personality variables, e.g.age, sex, cognitive ability, socio-economic class and education.
3) Sojourn experience – if sojourners are carefully introduced into a new society by close, sympathetic host culture friends, the evidence is that they will encounter fewer problems than if left to fend for themselves. This last point was developed by Furnham and Bochner (1979) when looking at culture shock.

Deaf people can also be seen as perpetrators of culture fatigue by hearing people. Not only do deaf young people and adults endure some degree of culture shock when seeking their identity as cultural and linguistic Deaf people, but my work with hearing parents has indicated they experience the same shock whilst bringing up their deaf child. The realisation that their child has a different view of the world means that they need to attempt to shift towards a more visual culture. Research into acculturalisation indicates that changes that are made to learn any new behaviour are extremely stressful for those making them. Hearing parents of deaf children need assistance in dealing with these stresses and tensions.

Mainstreamed and Oral deaf school children

I use the term "deaf" to mean anyone who is unable to hear human speech fully; this spans the audiological range from mild to profound deafness. However, the UK sign language community at present consists largely of profoundly Deaf users. This poses a problem to all deaf people who were mainstreamed and did not attend a sign language or sign system using unit or attended oral deaf schools. Not only were they not exposed to BSL but they may consider that they are not "deaf-enough" to belong to this community. At heart they know, although this may be repressed, that they are not fully at home in hearing communities. They may give inappropriate responses and, also, because their speech is intelligible they are not seen as being deaf by either hearing or deaf people. However, if one is born deaf with "useful hearing" it is easy to give the impression that one can hear more than is actually heard. This, logically speaking, leads one on to feel that one is hearing. "I don't think of you as deaf," say hearing people. This is seen as a complement, but actually reinforces the Catch 22 situation "think hearing" people are in. It is hard to break the cycle. "It is an achievement to realise one is not necessarily who others take one to be. Such awareness of discrepancy between self-identity (being for one-self), and being-for-others is painful," says Laing.(1969)

With respect to hard of hearing children, as they are called in Sweden, Swedish educationist/bilingual language planners are considering whether hard of hearing children should have sign language as L2. Hearing through hearing aids gives access, albeit partial, to spoken language as first language (L1). It will be interesting to note whether Swedish spoken language will affect their acquisition of sign language – this is often said in reverse, with no foundation.

Conclusion

To acquire any language one must have language models. Since Avram Naom Chomsky(1957) has published "Syntactic Structures", which proved to be a turning point in 20th century linguistics, there has been an ongoing debate about innate ability to acquire and decode language from babyhood. Behaviourists, such as Skinner, assume that babies are clean slates upon which language has to be imparted. Whichever theory applies, all children require language input. The best way for deaf children to become bilingual is for them to be exposed to native users of two languages. In so doing, the child is also exposed to two sets of cultural experiences. In this way deaf children can learn from an early age what it is like to be a deaf child and, consequently, a Deaf adult, whilst at the same time learning some of the mores and norms of hearing cultures. We can identify in part with the vast range of hearing groups. It widens our scope, our interests and belief systems. Socialisation is a natural process for any child, as should Deaf socialisation be for deaf children. There are several befriending schemes such as the Family project in Blackburn, Lancashire, formally introducing Deaf adults to deaf children in their homes as befrienders. "Permission to be deaf" from parents, family and wider society should be granted at a much earlier age than is often the case now, where it is only granted in early adulthood or even later, if at all.

To conclude, deaf people are not attracted to each other simply because of majority group pressure, in that we are forced to be together. It is far more than this. It is the need to know who one is. Being with other Deaf people makes us alive to our uniqueness as a Deaf person and also as a member of a unique group.

Bilingualism is, therefore, the master key towards the acquisition of a positive Deaf self-identity. This leads on to the development of healthy self-esteem, and to feelings of self worth and confidence. It is a vital key to us being able to be truly ourselves.

Jill Jones
September 1994
Revised 2003.

In this language for the eye

Hold a tree in the palm of your hand
Or topple it with a crash
Sail a boat on finger waves
Or sink it with a splash.
From your fingertips see a frog leap
At a passing butterfly.
The word becomes a picture
In this language for the eye.

Follow the sun from rise to set
Or bounce it like a ball.
Catch a fish in a fishing net
Or swallow bones and all.
Make traffic scurry and aeroplanes fly
And people meet and part
The word becomes reality
In this language of the heart.

Unknown author

9 *Memories of days in mainstream schools*

I was born with a good memory and, although during my first three years of life I had no experience hearing spoken English and no examples of adult British Sign Language, I remember my nursery days very clearly.

Now at twenty years of age, I look back and see myself in the nursery unit and class as a boy, small for his age who wanted to look into everything and find out how the toys worked. I had to wear two large hearing aids on my chest and the harness hurt my shoulders. In school a large Phonic Ear radio aid was placed on my chest and the sound I experienced from all the aids was an irritating scratching noise, like the feeling when you rub a board with your finger nails.

In the infant unit it was a similar situation, being expected to hear with a powerful radio aid when all I heard was a screechy noise, and having to follow spoken English which did not make sense when all I could do was try to lip-read sentences I had not heard. This caused some friction at home when my mother tried to make me wear the aids because she explained there would be problems at school if I did not wear it. She did not realise that the aids gave me no help at all in hearing the teacher.

One day I was playing in the infant school playground when I fell over and my Phonic Ear fell apart. The battery compartment separated from the aid and I could not get it back together again. We went back to the unit and I found the teacher was using the radio microphone but I received no noise; all was peaceful and quiet and I could concentrate better on the visual information.

Fortunately in the infant unit was another profoundly deaf pupil whose mother, father and brother were deaf. She would sign to me and, I realise now that my British Sign Language began to develop properly when I was five years old. We would sign fast and the adults could not follow, so our conversation could be humorously critical of our teachers. I enjoyed the infant unit, the maths and written work, and playing with deaf and hearing children even though the oral method was applied and the speech went completely over my head.

At seven years of age I moved to a junior unit where sign supported English was used. Some of the signs did not make sense and I became quite angry when hand shapes and placement were being used in a very peculiar way. At times I became bored and ventured out into the town to look at the shops. This caused problems as the staff insisted I stay on the school premises. School was becoming a prison and I felt restricted in the opportunities to learn.

I remember one Christmas-time that I removed the central strips which explode from the crackers in the unit. It was funny to watch the surprised faces of the partially hearing and hearing children and staff, whilst my profoundly deaf classmates behaved as usual.

At home my uncle had provided me with an Atari computer, and at the age of seven, I understood how to use this computer in different ways. My father obtained piles of lovely well-illustrated books from a next door neighbour, so at home I had lots to do, working the computer and looking at all the books. My grandmother bought a TV with teletext, so by the age of eleven I had a bedroom equipped for me to learn visually through programmes on Science, Nature, Geography on TV, word processing and games on the computer and interesting pictures and diagrams in the books which included encyclopaedias and books of knowledge showing how life began, how civilisation developed and the nature of the universe.

When I look back, living at home was an advantage because my family helped organise my bedroom as a study and they were there for me to show and discuss things I saw. At no time did I wish to leave my hearing family and go to a residential school for deaf children. My sisters are hearing but we developed our own sign system and got along well.

When I moved to the secondary unit, there were serious problems. The unit work was boring and the communicators who went with me to lessons did not sign very well. I enjoyed Information Technology lessons, but History Geography and Science were rather repetitive and slow. I took some of my books to school but there was no one with good enough BSL to follow topics through with me. Consequently I knowingly became disruptive.

For example, the window on the unit door had been covered up, so at playtimes we could not see who was in the room. I would kick the door and run up the corridor to see who would look out. In fact the door became quite damaged. Once I ,with two friends set off a fire extinguisher to see what reaction it might cause. Even now I consider it very funny, just like a Laurel and Hardy film. It is a pity the humour was not appreciated by others. Eventually at age fourteen, after several suspensions, the headmaster permanently excluded me and I had to find another school to take me.

I did not want to go to a school for deaf children because I was used to living in a hearing family and attending a hearing school. I spent about two months working with Sandra Dowe, home tutor mostly at her house where she had teletext TV, video camera, a 486 computer and some photographic equipment. Again the TV programmes were more informative to me as a deaf student than sitting in a classroom trying to follow lessons which were often visually boring.

After negotiations with a local upper school/community college, I was given a place, but was allowed to design my own timetable. This included following GCSE photography a year early at a local college of FE, and Science, Maths and Geography in the upper school. I had to do RSA English literacy as part of the National Curriculum, but at the same time Sandra booked me into BSL stage 1 and 2 classes at the college of FE.

I must admit I was not happy about doing BSL because I felt I did not need it. However since then I realised that the qualification is useful, and, who knows, I may help others to learn BSL in a more organised way.

The photography was interesting because it allowed me to experiment with cameras, developing and printing. Sandra also followed the course, but our strengths were obviously very different. I had more ideas regarding the visual aspect of the course, whilst Sandra enjoyed reading about the history of photography. Sandra bullied me into doing the assignment work, making me select relevant passages from textbooks to which I added my comments by signing and she translated into English which accompanied my illustrations. When it came to the exam, I gained more marks for my practical work whereas Sandra overtook me on the theory, especially the history.

Readers may think I was isolated, the only deaf student in an upper school, but I made friends and they attended lunchtime signing classes, so school life was not too bad. Sandra tried to bring in deaf adults to converse with me but I didn't feel I needed them.

Then in October 1995 Sandra, liaising with the careers department of my school and the local authority, instigated work experience for me at Barnfield College, Luton shadowing an IT technician. At first she came with me and organised a communicator to support me. After a few days the technician, other staff and students began to use visual ways of communicating with me, so Sandra withdrew and the communicator came only when I felt it necessary. I knew this was the work I wanted to do when I left school. Unfortunately it ended in November and I had to concentrate on my GCSE work.

In the Spring of 1996 Sandra and I followed the Computer Literacy and Information Technology level 1 course (CLAIT for short) at Barnfield College , and this was quite interesting.

In this situation, Sandra and I changed roles. She needed so much help knowing so little about computers that I had to share my time between doing the course work and showing her very basic operations. I quite enjoyed being in the driving seat for a change. It was through contacts with the IT staff at the college that I knew my next step would be following a full time BTEC computer studies course. The entrance requirements were a minimum of four GCSE subjects at C grade or above.

In the Summer of 1996 we awaited the GCSE results. It was a time to celebrate four C grades in Geography, Photography and a double Science award. During the next three years I studied computer related subjects.

Sometimes I wonder if my school days would have been different had I been hearing. The lessons and examinations I experienced are organised for hearing students. Is this fair? When I took control of my home tuition and GSCE school timetabling my learning became more effective. It is easier when you are older to state what you want. I could not tell my nursery and infant teachers what I wanted but did indicate my needs through behaviour. It may have been easier had my teachers been deaf like me. One day I hope to be in the position to assist deaf children learning IT at school to help adapt lessons to suit their ways of learning. Meanwhile I work as an ICT technician in an upper school/community college assisting hearing students and hope to gain teaching qualifications to teach both hearing and deaf students.

Simon Douglas
January 2000

When I'm at school people always look at me and my ears and I don't like it.

When I'm at school I'm fine and I'm well settled in. I have lots of new friends and they help me with my work. I have lots of SNA's helping me as well in the lessons. I have different SNA's sometimes. I feel different to all the other pupils because sometimes I can't hear them talking. I don't like it when I stutter because it makes me feel embarrassed. I like History because the teacher is really nice. My friends always help me in lesson and when I talk to them they don't ignore me. I'm pleased that I chose Farnley Park but I miss my other friends from Birchfield Primary. I like my mates at Farnley Park High, they are really kind to me. I like the teachers as well.

Josie
Aged 13

Here I am

Here I am, arrived at last,
Despite the rocky, sordid past.
I am Deaf; I've accepted this
Despite dissension, and the wish

To die at he whim of my own hand
Because no-one could understand.
I am D and little d
The two d/Ds live inside of me.

With hearing I am proud D
And fight them not to control me,
Mould into a hearing woman
For that's an impossible plan.
With my Deaf counterparts
I want to be Deaf with all my heart,
But will they let me be a D
When I'm not Deaf culturally?

Other cultures let sojourners
Learn and live with their new partners
In countries strange, new scenery,
Foreign smells, languages, finery.
We deaf mainstreamers live at home
But our land is not our own,
As we struggle to converse
And be part of our universe.

We want to be Deaf, and to be free
Of all this confused uncertainty.

Jill Jones
1st January 2000

10   *Technology and its affect on deaf identity development*

Cochlear implantation has created much controversy amongst the Deaf community: currently social research is being conducted into the non-medical aspects of cochlear implantation. Hearing aids, titanium implants, radio aids and other auditory aids have not aroused such passion. Why is this? These aids are the subject of this discussion paper.

Normalisation

It has been largely accepted by the Deaf community that, without becoming bilingual and bicultural, the deaf child can be harmed by cochlear implantation, because they prevent them being Deaf. My own view is that hearing aids and other hearing aided technology, i.e. loops, are equally powerful in the normalisation process. They are essential weapons without which deaf children cannot become "think-hearing" deaf people. The normalisation of deaf children is, in essence, hearing imperialism. To retain the status quo, hearing ness is the only status: anything other has to be inferior. It is a fascinating study of power which is further compounded by the "audist society", as Harlan Lane(1993) refers to it, dividing deaf people. This has resulted in the Deaf community marginalising "think-hearing" deaf people as "not-really-deaf", so that they have to live in limbo between two cultures.

Betty Friedan(1963) wrote of women in America who were not economically exploited but who felt their lives were empty and did not know who they were or who they wanted to become. She asked how to organise politically around a sense of emptiness? In attempting to normalise deaf people, we become non-people who think we are hearing but of course are not. Part of the power dynamics is to depersonalise people so that they have no clear identity.

Aids for disabled people

Symbol canes for blind people obviously serve the purpose of drawing attention to the visual disability and long canes act as a mobility aid. The wheelchair is a different mobility device to enable the physically disabled person to get around.

There can be no doubt that equipment of this nature enables partial access but at the same time ensures that the disability is prominent so that the identity of the disabled person is not in question.

Hearing aids seem to fulfil a different function which is to make the deaf person appear "normal". Behind-the-ear aids are discreet and cochlear and titanium implants are usually hidden, as far as possible, by the wearer.

Hearing aided technology is used in order to supplement any residual hearing. Deaf people do not function in all social situations, even with hearing aids, as they do not restore or give hearing where none exists. Even the most sophisticated aids cannot enable us to discriminate all sounds, perfectly locate directional sounds or hear in noisy situations. It, therefore, follows that we usually cannot hear in groups or with background noise, though one-to-one can be manageable. Some deafened adults appear to function well with aids, as they struggle to retain their lifelong identity.

Deaf children are in a constant learning state which makes their needs different from deafened adults. This is one of the reasons DEX advocates that all deaf children should be allowed to be bilingual and bicultural.

Monolingual deaf children

Hearing aids subtly give the message that it is taboo to be deaf. As the result of advertising by hearing aid companies about "hidden hearing" and "pop-in aids", society, already misled by our invisible disability, is further misinformed.

The deaf child absorbs these messages day by day, and the routine of putting on and the taking off of hearing aids also means that the aid feels like an appendage. An aid that is so integral a part of one's body does not feel alien.

Parents of deaf children are advised to persist with hearing aid training, despite the deaf child's dislike of the foreign body in the ear, the strange emissions, the sudden loud sounds and muffled, constant background blur. Whilst working at NDCS and in social work I am still informed by many parents about the methods used by professionals, and which are emulated by parents, to cajole or enforce deaf children to wear their hearing aids. The techniques range from "pin down" and physical force, to threatening to send the deaf child to a special school for children with learning disabilities. The children are told that they will not speak or be clever or belong, that they will be sent away or be punished.

There are many and varying reasons why deaf children or young people may not want to wear hearing aids. A deaf baby may find the mould intrusive in the ear, the sounds startling after months of quiet. Hearing people can tend to assume that we should be grateful to receive the cacophony of sounds that surround us! Throughout childhood the hearing aid offers no relief from background jumble so the deaf child may use the hearing aid as a means of rebellion, in the same way as a toddler's refusal to be potty trained or eat.

"If the infant does object to being put on the pot," says Penelope Leach(1974), "and his mother tries to insist she will very quickly find that she has joined in a battle in which there is no way for her to win."

During adolescence the deaf young person, in addition to coping with the negatives of hearing aids, can become very self-conscious about wearing them, feeling different and, therefore, unacceptable to his peer group. It can, again, become a sticking point between the deaf young person and adults and a means of reinforcing the generation differences.

It is crucial that hearing aid usage, or non-usage as the case may be, is balanced against the deaf child's general needs. Adolescents' social behaviour, according to Sandstrom (1966), "implies social initiation and development, which are of fundamental importance if a person is to be at home in the adult world." If deaf young people are forced to wear hearing aids at the expense of their social development then this has to be abusive.

Abuse

By the time the deaf young person reaches adulthood the "adaptive behaviour", has culminated in learned responses to hearing aid usage. The Deaf community now sign that wearing an aid is similar to solvent abuse. Deaf people become addicted and find they cannot manage without them. Personally, I have experienced "cold turkey" (to use a probably outdated '60's phrase). This is the fear of not being able to communicate without an aid, panic attacks and cravings to replace the aid in the ear. Gradually the fear subsided over about 6 years as I began slowly withdrawing the aid, using it less and less and relying more on visual aids and BSL interpretation. Now I only use it when strictly necessary, at work with family and friends I do not lip-read well.

At work I do feel ambivalent about being more "think-hearing", for it is necessary for survival and particularly for my family, as they must be fed and clothed. Prostitutes describe the same philosophy in working to support their children.

DEX members and Deaf friends have explained their similar feelings, of panic, lack of control over their environment without hearing aid batteries or aids. Adam Walker, a Deaf mature student, had a bet with a fellow student that he could manage without his aids for a month. He won the bet but it was one of the worse experiences in his life. He found that hearing friends started to shun him, but on the other hand, others became more deaf aware and took more trouble to include him. His tutorials and lectures became problematic but new ways were found to replace stressful hearing related methods. His lip-reading skills, like those who do not rely too much on residual hearing, improved.

Another profoundly Deaf friend says he cannot walk without his aid on; he feels that it rectifies his balance problem. Common amongst us all is the uncertainty of not being able to monitor our voices without an aid, but this is hard, anyway, to do with it on.

As with many artificial devices the body adapts and can create false illusions. The pain or discomfort of wearing a hearing aid, in the same way as an artificial limb, can be diminished if the brain is active with other things. Loud or background noises have to be shut out or they are too intrusive.

Long term affects of Hearing Aid Usage

It is common to find amongst the Deaf community Deaf people who have tinnitus. There is general feeling that this is likely to be due to wearing hearing aids and radio aids for long periods. There appears to be no research into this phenomenon. The British Society of Audiologists or the Hearing Research Trust at Nottingham has done nothing to investigate this, to my knowledge. I have both tinnitus and hypercusis (sensitive hearing), so it is possible that my views will be considered to be biased. With 46 years of wearing hearing aids behind me, however, there could well be foundation in our theory. Sensitive hearing and tinnitus make hearing aids even harder to use, so it is hardly surprising that I have flung them out of the car window several times. What may be odd is that I have always retrieved them from gutter or verge. It demonstrates the love-hate relationship with the aid, and ambivalence.

Testing for hearing aid prescriptions is another area of concern, but I do not have enough evidence to do anything but mention it in this discussion document. In my personal and professional experience, testing of hearing leaves a lot to be desired. In one particular case, now lasting 8 years, the mother of two deaf children has fought hard for audiologists to accept that her older deaf child has non-organic deafness. Her child functions as a deaf child and, as such, should be enabled to access special education and services for deaf children. Hearing aids are passports because audiologists are gatekeepers to services. The deaf young woman, as she now is, has gone throughout her entire schooling without any support and, indeed, been accused of pretending to be deaf, whilst her mother is said to be responsible for child abuse.

I wonder who the real perpetrators here are. This is not one isolated incident, as deaf children with so-called mild or moderate losses are forgotten in schools and their needs not addressed in their homes.

Hearing testing divides deaf children into "haves" and "have nots": those who can hear and those who cannot with hearing aids and this is slowly but surely killing off the Deaf community and our language. There is no surer way of deaf eugenics than the aiding of deaf children and normalisation. Harlan Lane(1993) has this to say about cochlear implantation, which is no different from any auditory aiding, apart from the serious medical intervention required:

"Among the biological means for regulating and, ultimately, eliminating deaf culture and language and community, cochlear implants have historical antecedents, then, in medical experimentation on deaf children and reproductive regulation on deaf adults."

Bilingualism and Biculturalism

"Bi-bi" as this is now called, is already happening in some local education authorities, but even there, much work is needed to ensure that families with deaf children are supported in becoming Deaf/hearing families. Being a bicultural family is a delicate task, in the face of hearing socialisation. Bilingualism entails spoken language development takes place as well as BSL learning. How do we ensure that hearing aided technology does not discourage Deaf identity development whilst, at the same time, create a "think-hearing" one?

Getting the balance right can only is achieved by allowing the deaf child to own the hearing aid or implant and to use it when comfortable or appropriate. For spoken language development and hearing socialisation, it is obviously important that the deaf child is encouraged to wear aids but it should never be at the expense of the deaf child's wishes. Each deaf child should be gently taught to value hearing aids' benefits as well as their limitations. In so doing the deaf child learns to understand her own deafness, should be able to sign and talk freely about being Deaf and to move between cultures and languages. Hearing aided technology, used sensitively and with empathy from hearing parents and professionals can contribute to the deaf child's sense of belonging to hearing cultures, within the limits of aided hearing, and also to belong to Deaf culture. In this way the deaf child will feel valued and safe.

In "Dibs: in Search of Self" Axline (1964), Dibs finds his self worth:

"He had learnt to understand his feelings. He had learnt how to cope with them and to control them. Dibs was no longer submerged under his feelings of fear and anger and hatred and guilt. He had become a person in his own right. He had found a sense of dignity and self respect."

Deaf children are taught by society that they are second-class citizens and this, naturally, can only belittle them in their own eyes and make them feel worthless. DEX members and allies recount the same story, of lack of confidence, feelings of inadequacy, depression, competitiveness, overcompensation (eating disorders, etc), physical and mental ill health, and history of relationship problems and so on. This is anecdotal but we hope that DEX research will show evidence of the results of normalisation.

As Sula Wolff(1969) says:

"Moreover, recovery from gross deprivation or distortion of the socialisation process in early life takes many years."

Cyril Burt (1944) further expounds this point, which is reinforced in much work done by child psychologists and psychiatrists.

"They are the children who from their earliest days have lacked those essentials to their well being, the loss of which nothing in this world can compensate for. They are love and security."

It is essential that deaf children are loved for themselves and allowed to be Deaf. This is regardless of audiological measurements, aiding, cause or onset of deafness. Parents must have deep understanding of the positives and negatives of auditory aids, encouraged to use visual aids and supported in becoming bilingual and bicultural families. To achieve that all professionals must have the same goals in supporting families in this understanding, and must move away from their ethnocentric view of deafness.

Roger Green, (1990) audiologist, wrote:

"An audiologist working with the hearing impaired child needs to be a versatile member of the rehabilitation team...The aid itself provides a door through which that child can enter a hearing world, but every child needs to be helped through that door. For that to happen the audiologist must work in close liaison with parents, teachers, doctors, and all the other care-givers involved with the child. Only then will he have provided the child with his/her best chance of overcoming the handicap of his/her deafness."

There is a great deal to do to overcome the handicap of hearing attitude. In addition deaf people need to understand the value, but also the drastic limitations, of hearing aided technology and to be united in empathising the diverse effects that technology has on the hearing mechanism. This lack of empathy disembowels us when professionals question that deaf people have different views, and divides us. Until we begin to identify with each others' common problems with aids, and understand the power that normalisation has over us, then deaf children will continue to be abused.

As Harlan Lane says: "If the birth of a deaf child is a priceless gift, then there is only one cause for rejoicing, as at the birth of a black child or an Indian one."

ONE MONTH BET

A student 's account of his endeavour to live without hearing aids for a month after being told he couldn't.

I am a deaf undergraduate student studying Peace Studies. I met someone one night in January who had a theory that deaf people couldn't live without hearing aids. This theory was based on an assumption that born deaf people once diagnosed at birth (6 – 9 months) were given hearing aids thus having to live with it all their lives. It's like an addiction to it. In my case I was given my first aids at 9 months old and have lived with it from when I wake up in the morning or afternoon to closing my eyes in late evening or early morning if it is a good party! The only times I don't wear them is when I ride my motorcycle or someone says "Oi! You owe me a fiver!" or "Have you done your essay yet?" I've never really taken them out and rely on them, especially with the Northern accent. It is incomprehensible to this Southerner, and Maggie Thatcher denied the existence of the North/South divide?!

That night while heavily intoxicated I challenged my friend's theory and made a bet with him for a fiver that I would live without the hearing aid for one month starting from 10th January This is the account :

The first two weeks have been sheer hell! I have to remind my mates to open their months wider and speak slower than usual. They do forget from time to time. Another assumption about hearing aids is that you can then hear like anyone else. In fact it only amplifies sounds in all range of tones so that you can pick up background hubbub as well in noisy places like rowdy pubs. An average human being like yourself, if you are average, can filter this and hear what you want to. In my case my hearing is like picking up static sounds so I generally lip-read. There ye go!

Returning to the month's experiment, some people would get irritated and lack patience especially when they would have to repeat things like a tape recorder if I misunderstood them. They sometimes reached a point of insanity and end up having to flap their arms and dance about in a frenzy! Some though cling on and are patient and I have to be patient with them and calm them down (no, not with tranquillisers). Lecturers at Peace Studies were patient enough, surprising compared with others.

The last two weeks weren't that bad, people have learnt to be patient with me (haemorrhage or heart attack in surprise). I've improved my lip-reading in a big way. For the first time since moving to Bradford I've managed to understand the Northern accent!

One mate who gave me details of his experiences with me said that he built up his understanding with me in terms of communications.

When I was wearing the aid he could attract my attention by calling. In the days without aids he found himself having to walk up to tap my shoulder! When out at night I was quieter rather than in a talkative way and have improved my perception towards the end of the month's transitional phase.

A month later and I've started to see that science can be golden! The conclusion is that I only wear aids sometimes when I do really need it. I saw my mate again and won that fiver which I quickly traded in for beers!

Adam Walker
February 1995

Shadow

The past has passed; let the pain die.
I stand at forked left/right road,
Within me still the fading cry,
Because it was an onerous load.

Who really knew me? Really knew,
Who was my own age and kind,
Through life, and childhood, with me grew -
And understood what was in my mind?

Shadow-person, I was not me.
In hearing footsteps always near;
Tried to wear false identity,
"Not really deaf", for I could hear.

Those who hear, how can they relate
To shadowlands; half heard sounds;
Ephemeral waves we translate
Into syntax, to verbs and nouns?

And so I search for those between
Two worlds – the twilight zone
That lies t'wixt those who hear and glean,
And those who are as deaf as stone.

On this recent road, like minds I've met,
Twilight Deaf friends, we can compare -
We've come on different roads – and yet
Joint dreams we can exchange and share.

I've journeyed long with different minds,
The road was hard, yet my love so free,
I want to journey with my own kind -
Learn to be Deaf and to be me.

I was trained to be a selfless soul,
I feel so selfish, so self aware.
Over two score years, my strength unfolds,
And my Deaf self was waiting there.

I've severed the shadow; we bleed
Apart, in silent agony,
Our distance overcomes the need
To be the pair we used to be.

I can't reject my hearing friends
Who love me, thought they knew me -
Warm thanks to all whose love transcends
Our difference in identity.

Each of us has to know our truth;
Where we came from, who we are -
Can't hide from it as we mistook
Hearing people for our guiding star.

Take me to the sanctuary
Where people are who're just like me,
Gives us inner strength; now will there be
Welcoming hands to the Deaf country?

Jill Jones
August 1994

11   *Are you stupid as well as Deaf*

I am 27 years old and partially Deaf and also have a severe speech impediment. I would like to tell you about my experience of a Deaf child who went through the mainstream school and how important it is to get access into the Deaf community. As a child the first school I went to was an infant school and was the only Deaf child in the school and had no support of any kind. I wore one of the hearing aids you clip onto your chest and it was the first time many of the children had seen one so they used to have turns pulling the wires leading to my ears and turning the volume control up and down, I was too timid to do anything about it and was left out of many of the school activities such as school plays and swimming. I was also pushed aside by many of the teachers due to my communication problem. I can remember one time that a teacher was shouting at me because I did not hear her telling me to do something so she shouted to me in front of the class "are you stupid as well as Deaf" and I ran out of the school in tears and was punished for it. Many times, I was made to feel inferior and stupid just because I could not communicate like the other children and when I moved to secondary school there was worse to come.

On the first day I was degraded, in registration the teacher was calling the names out and I was sat at the back of the classroom as all the intelligent kids sat at the front and just because I never heard the teacher call out my name I was called ignorant which the other kids had a great laugh at my expense. It was the infant school all over again as I was the only Deaf pupil in the school and my speech impediment did not help much. When I started to wear a behind the ear hearing aid I grew my hair long to hide the fact that I was Deaf as I was made to feel ashamed of my disability. There was never a day went by I wasn't degraded or humiliated, had friends at the school but they were never really close friends, and didn't understand my disability. All the anger and frustration built up in me, and started getting into fights and playing truant to avoid school and it gave me a bad reputation which followed me when I left school. I left school with no qualifications because I wanted to leave as quickly as I could and was a very bitter person with all the anger and frustration in me, I thought all my problems would be over when I left but I was wrong. There I was in the big wide world with no identity, I wasn't an hearing person and wasn't a Deaf person. About I year after going on training schemes and getting kicked off them I got involved with a group of youths and started breaking the law just to get them to like me and everytime I did something bad they would pat me on the back and I thought at last I can do something to make me feel part of a crowd. Things got worse as I started to go to football matches and with all the anger and frustration I had from my school days came out and was joining in with the hooligans which eventually led to being banned from the ground for life.

I then turned to drinking and I would sit alone in a pub and intentionally get drunk and try and forget about my disability and would avoid talking to people as I thought all people were the same and would make fun of me. Then I started getting depressed after going in and out of dead end jobs and things started getting serious, I would carry a knife with me because I hated people and if anyone just looked at me I would start an argument (when I was drunk I could speak more fluently) and end up fighting then I was getting searched by police and would end up in court on knife offences and one time when a group of men started making fun of me I just thought that's it enough is enough and ended up maliciously wounding one of the men. So again I was in court and I explained to my solicitor about why I was so bitter and the judge took pity on me and gave me twelve months probation and that is when things started looking up. I realised how serious the problem was of having all the anger and frustration inside of me due to people not being aware of my communication problem. I went to my GP to ask him about help available for my communication difficulty, so he put me in touch with a woman who was involved in the local Deaf club and she invited me to the AGM and from then on the members of the club helped me by teaching me sign language and communication skills which helped my speech because when I sign I can talk fluently and now sixteen months on I am the Secretary of the Deaf Club and also a volunteer at a Deaf Advice Service and I am a trained Deaf Awareness teacher, so I teach nurses, doctors, magistrates etc.. basic sign language and deaf awareness. I strongly feel that if I went to a Deaf school or had support in the mainstream schools. Things also would have been very different, if I had accessed earlier the Deaf community as this has totally changed my life. I would never have thought of the things I have achieved two years ago. There will be many more Deaf children and adults out there who have gone through mainstream schools who need the help and support I got as they have no identity what so ever and they are the unfortunate people that society discards.

Shaun Thomas

12   *Hyacinth's story*

When I was 3 years old deafness came. I went to deaf nurseries, deaf infants, then deaf group into hearing junior, (then this is a terrible mistake) went to hearing school, the secondary school and I was the only one deaf. But I had Asian hearing friends. I don't know how it happen, leaving school into hearing world, I did not have any information about deaf people or where they go. I was brought up in a hearing family I am the youngest, I had terrible brother and sister who had no patience with me, like monster, out of control to yell at me.

Anyway, to hearing world and hearing people, to college with deaf group, R.S.A. and Maths and English, I pass, but the hearing school I failed just general studies grade 5, better off in deaf school, understand myself with deaf students. So Y.T.S. employment with hearing people was terrible experience, I was with wrong people. Every job I was in, I resign because I feel discriminate by hearing people.

I feel this generation's dislike of the difference, and call names because of our hearing problems, being pushed around saying things to get you out of the job. In hearing world I feel reject by them, seem not interested in me, especially at church for 15 years. I was loving and supportive, but people around did not understand me to show some friendship, all I hear (in greeting) "hello, how are you? Goodbye" with hands shaking, but I don't get much call (phone) or visits to my home. I visit some friends, but they don't so I am surprised what went wrong, so I move to another church make more friends, is the same situation.

What happened is my family did not have encouragement to help me, the real me, and the people behind me, it very sad that I live alone for 5 years now so lonely and now I go to deaf club, because just at 30 years of age, just now I begin to realise the real me, why I was with wrong people, for so long, and now I have little few deaf friends which I need to get back where I belong, having friends who are deaf, and can communicate with me, outings, theatre, sports and club, when I go to deaf club, it full, finish 12 midnight, they talk about where they been lately and work and family. Deaf people really enjoy themselves, my life could be lots better if I was with them. Please do not let the deaf children suffer what I went through.

Hyacinth McDonald

13 Cognition and deafness

Talk given at Plymouth University, April 1997.

Introduction

Adam Walker was a Researcher at Bristol University, Dept CDS, doing MPhil in the effects of mainstream education on deaf children and now employed at Durham University. He co-founded DEX.

Policy of Mainstreaming

In 1995 93.7% of deaf children were in mainstream schools compared to 64% in 1981. The 1981 Education Act made provision for the decline of deaf residential schools with the conditional integration of deaf children to mainstream schools: this was usually expressed in terms of equal rights.

The terms integration and assimilation are both used loosely by educationalists to mean different levels of integration. although abolishing segregation is used by the 1981 Education Act to close down special schools for the deaf, in order for the deaf children to assimilate with their hearing peers. Conversely this has had the effect, at the same time of segregating the deaf children from their own Deaf community.

Integration became a challenge to create opportunities for meaningful interaction and a right to a broad and balanced curriculum, at the expense of deaf children's identity development and social education. The theory is that deaf children should have first hand experience of ordinary society and for society to have first hand experience of them. *Originally, the idea of equal opportunity human rights for minority groups was adopted as the justification.*

Audiologists , teachers, and parents of deaf children were encouraged to consider greater individual integration. the government have, since 1983, replaced the term "deaf" with "Children with Special Educational Needs" (SEN) which now hinders our attempts to determine how many deaf children are in school today.

Deaf children's special needs were treated within a pathological approach rather than social /psychological approach, whilst we have Deaf identity groups as a linguistic minority and a thriving community which has a rich culture. They are older profoundly Deaf people: younger deaf people are not joining in significant numbers. Yet we know that these same Deaf people can have poor reading skills , low academic achievement and poor jobs. The roots of this problem lie in the theories and practical evidences pointed to deaf children's educational placement, and it is the impact of these theories which need to be assessed in this research. (Walker. A 1995).

Methods for integration or mainstreaming have been rudimentary for years. There is no set standard to which type to use . Simply, integration for deaf people is taken by hearing people to mean "normalisation".

"The definition of normalisation: that the hearing -impaired child should in all respects be helped to be as like a hearing child as possible, i.e. should be "adapted". The ultimate aim would therefore be normal speech, comprehension by the least obvious means possible-unobtrusive hearing aids, lip reading, handouts. The child would be expected to be treated on equal terms academically, socially etc with his/her peers. The ultimate form of the paradigm would allow, for example, no obvious help from a teacher of the deaf, and certainly no use of sign language" (Sellars. M./Palmer. B. Etal. (1992)

Mainstreaming of deaf children is on the grounds that is oriented not towards the educational needs, but towards the reinforcement of the dominant ideology of equality of access to educational structural inequalities, – the sociology of culture, the sociology of language is logically inseparable from a sociology of education.

Patterns of Mainstreaming Provision

1. Individual and unsupported placement where the deaf child is placed in the classroom alongside hearing peers with or without a hearing aid or radio aid and with no other deaf peers in the school.

2. Individual and supported placement
   a) where a teacher of deaf children or the Head of Hearing Impaired Services gives advice to the school about how to teach more appropriately.
   b) where a teacher of deaf children visits to teach the deaf child. This could be once, trebly, monthly or weekly.
   c) where a non-teaching assistant supports the deaf child. This person has different job titles in each local authority (classroom assistant, teaching support staff, etc). This can be several hours

a week or full time. A teacher of deaf children can also advise the assistant and other members of staff. All above can still entail that the deaf child has no deaf peers,either in the same class or within different year groups.

3. The same provision as (2) but there are a few other deaf children in school. Unless they are in the same classroom (which is usually discouraged) they rarely meet.

4. Resourced provision (or unit)

   a) mostly based within a classroom, but brought to the Hearing Impaired Unit(or Department) for specialised teaching with a teacher of deaf children, usually for English or foreign languages, or English based subjects i.e. History. This can be once a week or more often. Although there is a deaf peer group, they are usually dispersed throughout the school and rarely attend the same classes.

   b) based within the units but integrated into the school for certain subjects, usually P.E or Art. This type of mainstreaming is now extremely rare. This "school within school" approach is not viewed as integration, although the deaf community favours this, as well as education in deaf schools.

Communication methods used in mainstreaming

Practically all mainstreamed deaf children are expected to use the majority language, which is spoken. *Some local authorities offer units which use Total Communication (T.C.) as the teaching tool. Fairly recently, an impetus was given to the use of sign bilingualism in some places.*

Total Communication

This meant that the oral approach with emphasis on speech, lip-reading and auditory training, forms the basis of all communication, but signs (taken from the BSL) and finger spelling are used to support and reinforce the oral means as and where necessary. The use of signs takes the form of Signed English or Sign Supported English as appropriate, according to the situation.

Sign Bilingualism

Several local authorities provide bilingual education within mainstream units or schools. This again is though to be only suitable for profoundly deaf children and involves B.S.L. and English, which are used separately (and not simultaneously as in T.C.). This provides deaf children with fluent language from which to learn English, especially in the written form. It is also essential for bonding with other deaf children and Deaf adults and provides access to an identity group. From that their Deaf identity will develop as they identify with positive role models. As the school must employ Deaf adults to teach B.S.L., this provides deaf children with cultural role models too.

Mainstreamed children's behavioural needs

Each child is an individual in his or her own right with differing needs. There is a view that Deaf pupils should be involved in clarifying their own needs, as the professionals do not readily take into account of their needs and do not ask them what they want. Many schools have pupils representatives to air their own views, but deaf pupils do not have that kind of access.

There are two points I want to remind you of, regarding the complexity of communication and language, in academic and social areas:

1. Academically: whatever the input the teacher gives to children, the deaf child in the same class needs time to take it in. The complexity of language used can result in lack of comprehension, and in addition deaf children cannot hear all that is said in a classroom environment , even with aids. There is need for extra time with a deaf child in a hearing class. The amount of time that the deaf child is taking, results in delay and confusion.

2. Socially: if the deaf child is in a peer group of hearing children, the complexity of language usage amongst the children leads to the deaf child having problems in cognitive development and thus could not fit in social groups. As a result the child would either withdraw himself to quiet solitude or to aggressive social behaviour. This is illustrated in letters and contacts made through the Deaf Ex-Mainstreamers' Group.

Deaf pupils behave in different ways; as the child reaches secondary age, there is a balancing act between striving for "normality" as depending on intrusive support for survival becomes more difficult. Deaf children want to appear to be as normal as possible and they do not want to be singled out for special attention; do not always like to wear the bulky and visible looking radio aid, 'cos everyone stares'. Most do not like phonic ear, but prefer post -aural aids, because no one could see; there are many cases of adolescents rejecting or resenting their support teaching in mainstream, as they regard it as embarrassing and humiliating. Many refuse to wear radio aids, as they felt that emphasised their deafness. Deaf children often refuse to acknowledge their own deafness. There are cases of deaf individuals who have been known to refuse any contact with fellow deaf peers at school or in adult life. *"...he doesn't want to be seen to be like them , because 'they are regarded as stupid by his schoolmates, so he shrinks from this contact like the plague"* (Ladd.1981)

As deaf children are brought up to have equal status with hearing children, we are walking the fine line of 'how far should we have equality' and the views of 'liberty'.

Deaf children are working under considerable strain. Few are prepared to gain attention by asking teachers for further explanation if not understood. Therefore, the wish to keep a low profile is common practice. Parents and teachers speak with rueful exasperation of deaf children being 'their own worse enemy' by purposely giving the appearance of having understood when in fact they have not. Going up to the teacher more than usual can make the teacher really cross. How far can the child take it all in when attempting to lip-read a teacher (space and time) for comprehensive understanding?

Social integration is probably more problematic to achieve than academic integration, since it is less amenable to formal intervention and support services. Conversations can take place in: corridors, dining halls, playgrounds and classrooms. When children grow into the adolescent stages, it sets the deaf child apart from the hearing peer groups, especially when the group spend their playtime talking. For the deaf child is a big jump from being younger when engaging in running around games. So when deaf individuals attempt to socialise with hearing peers he often misses the meaning of jokes, quick remarks, and worse, cannot pick up whispers and nudges. At the adolescent stage, children need each other to identify with: clubs and gangs form, so lacking cognition can lead to either withdrawal to isolation or aggression. Adolescents need to interact into peer groups and friendships, and to develop or break them.

Some deaf children have no sense of belonging, either to the hearing community of the school, or to the Deaf community if one comes into contact with from time to time. Where a deaf child's speech is good, people do not realise how deaf the child could be.

Evidences have been collected in the last three years in the form of letters being sent to Deaf Ex-Mainstreamers' Group and contacts with deaf individuals illustrating the views of the adults who are former mainstreamers. This included visits to Deaf centres and Deaf youth

deaf children was impeded. Teachers were not SEN trained at teacher training courses, let alone even taught to use sign language. This applies especially to the teacher of deaf children. Some teachers, after teaching for many years, are having to learn sign language on the job in order to fulfil the educational needs of deaf children.

For teachers to adapt teaching strategies to cope, smaller classes are needed, especially since the implementation of the National Curriculum. Nowadays most secondary schools have 30 children within a class. For a teacher, time needed to be spent with each pupil is approx. 1 minute 30 seconds if the lesson time is on average 45 to 60 minutes. To make matters worse mainstreamed deaf children are being put into classrooms with their hearing peers as common practice and they need more time span attention, thus putting pressure on a teacher.

Another problem that deaf children have to face is the acoustic setting. Deaf children who are wearing hearing aids do not have the ability to block out background noise. The classroom can echo especially if it is not treated with carpets and Sound Fields, although again, this does not compensate for normal hearing. With 30 odd children, the deaf child would face a background of hubbub from children and teacher thus causing the deaf child having to strain to lip-read the teacher harder.

How can one devise cognitive strategies for deaf children? As evidenced around the country, some classrooms adopt the practice of employing NTAs to act as a go-between for deaf pupils and teachers. There is a view regarding the use of NTAs.

There have been cases of deaf children wanting to appear as normal as is humanly possible, and they do not want to be singled out for special attention."...the feeling of having 'a specialist' teacher makes him feel like a pampered mummy's boy" (Ladd. 1981).

Another view is the cohesive social interaction with fellow deaf peers is essential to develop complex communicative skills.

Look no ears! – she's not deaf

This story can never recapture the full details, and I take no real pleasure from recounting it, as I feel the sickness in my stomach – of memories which have recently, thankfully, been pushed into the dark recesses of my mind. I believe that mainstreaming has not only affected my life, but also my relationships and more crucially, my children. Of course, many factors are brought to play when bringing up children. If parents' behaviour, however, is said to influence children then it follows that if a parent has low feelings of self-worth, then it is very likely to affect their child's self-esteem development.

I believe that my mainstream education seriously limited my chances of having a healthy sense of self esteem as I was never treated as a Deaf person, but as a flawed hearing person. This has gone on to affect my own hearing children's development, and particularly my daughter, as her role model. For me, the extreme lack of self love and confidence, even self loathing, that has resulted from my education and upbringing has been with me all my life. I married two hearing men and have two beautiful adult hearing children: a son who is insecure and a daughter who struggles with depression and feelings of low self worth. I am angry about the effect my life has had on theirs, and the system that has produced this, probably more than I am angry about my own life.

I was a post-war time baby, born in 1946 when rations were in and money was scarce and Britain was beginning to rebuild. It was a cold winter, one of the coldest on record, so, like all babies at that time I wore fetching woollen bonnets. In the following hot summer, I was still put into cotton bonnets even in the house, for I was born with no ears. Treacher Collins Syndrome was only diagnosed eight years ago, but this was the cause of my middle ear deafness which was then, probably moderate. I have been told that I have lost some hearing and now have severe to profound deafness.

I had a loving family, working class conservatives, so although financially not well off, were aspiring and secure. For the first five years I was the apple of my grand father and father's eyes. Although I now know that my lack of ears had been a shock, naturally, their way of coping with it was to pretend that I did not have a problem. I had long and thick wavy hair, which was rolled into rags each night to crimp it into a mass of tumbling curls which hid my loss of ears. Despite the nightly process with rags and water pulling my scalp, I remember happiness. I believe I was diagnosed as being deaf at about the age of four or five years old, despite having no ears!

Being taken into hospital and waking up with my arm in splints so that I could not remove my bandages around my head, was the beginning of the sense of something happening to change this happiness. This was the first round of operations I had, which was the first of about ten. These included stapedectomy (or fenestration as it was then called), attempting to improve or cure my deafness. In addition was the plastic surgery to correct my tiny stumps for ears. On one side I only had an ear lobe, but now have a strange misshapen thing that is a mistaken identity of an ear, where the plastic surgeons seemed to have run out of plastic. The left hand one can hold a hearing aid. Many times I wish that they had run out of plastic for that one too!

I was fitted with a bone conduction body worn aid when I was five years old. These aids were first issued that same year to all deaf children in 1951.

I well remember, better than yesterday, being on the street outside the hospital with my father proudly asking me what I could hear. I have seen deaf children react in the same way to cochlear implants being switched on, amazement that there is sound, an initial reaction of shock. Some deaf children cry. I only remember the unpleasant roar of buses and cars rushing past, few as they were in those days, but have no sense of emotion to go with the recognition of a new sense, as it was such a totally unexpected experience. No-one had told my parents to switch off in loud situations or to ease me into getting used to it. It was assumed that it was something natural as it is for hearing people and which they can adjust automatically. This was, in actual event, a new chapter in my life after five years of muted sounds or silence.

I much later discovered that the local authority wanted me to attend the local special school for partially hearing children about twenty miles away. Because it was a boarding school my parents wanted me to attend the local hearing mainstream school. My hearing brother, then aged just seventeen years, was dispatched to the education office to plead my case, and he must have succeeded because I started at the local infant school on trial. This "trial" resulted in my spending the rest of my education in mainstream schools and college without any support and with no deaf peers at all.

I was one of the first to be completely mainstreamed throughout my education in such a fashion. I know of many of my age who attended mainstream schools, but also went to Deaf schools, usually because they were seen as not able to cope. This "oral failure" concept still survives to this day.

My other remaining clear memory of childhood are of towering school gates, and the physical dread and terror I daily felt on walking through each set : infant, junior and grammar schools alike. I felt physically sick and I wanted to turn and flee. I did abscond when I was in junior school from about eight or nine years of age. For someone who lived in such timidity and fear, this was a massive step to take, but I wandered about the streets in the vicinity, particularly hanging about the dancing school which was my main visual entertainment.

I tore up the letters about my absence from school and disposed of them down the grid in the street. Finally a letter must have been posted to my home because one day I was greeted by a very irate mother, who not only tore *me* to shreds but rattled my head against a cupboard for good measure. This persuaded me never to abscond again (or "sag", as we called it) or to lie. I was left, however, with a feeling of nausea and dread which I could no longer deal with by flight, but by internalisation and becoming introverted.

Bullying by teachers and hearing children was either physical or emotional and continued until I went to an all girls' grammar school. The teachers' attitude to me varied from not being aware that I was deaf, so treating me no differently, to those who actually singled me out as a trouble maker, usually for talking in class to find out what was happening. Their punishments ranged from hauling me out in full view of assemblies because I did not know the words to hymns or psalms, and making me stand next to the line of teachers still mouthing like a fish, or to standing in the corridor or behind the blackboard. Hours of wasted time, not knowing what was happening from outside or even within the classroom on punishments, but the grosser damage, and much more subtle, was not fully being aware during my education in all my time at school or in the college of further education. I cannot remember being physically beaten by staff, but that may have been because I was a girl

In the playground or at break time in class, I was plagued for my bulky hearing aid. I remember being chased home up the leafy streets of my suburban area, hot footed by boys and being cornered in a shop alleyway. The hearing aid box, brown leathered and with long straps, proved to be an ally as a weapon, as I slung it about my head and hurled it at my assailants. I think they did not trouble me again after that. I don't expect the aid worked though.

Throughout my education, and now in adulthood, I have been a loner. I was always on the fringe of peer groups, from infancy to now. I was a veteran "hanger-on", learnt the skill to an art. I perfected the skill of looking as if I understood, of nodding, laughed when the others did and said as little as possible. I had no opinions anyway, as I had insufficient knowledge on which to base opinions. I soon knew when I was not wanted and moved on to watch more activity. This art of being a part of things but still very much alone, has a huge price to play on self worth. Not feeling part of the group, or belonging leads to all sorts of pain, in different guises. These materialised throughout my life as a woman who loved too much. I was the one who bought sweets to school to give away, to buy love, and the one who always ran to help when a child had fallen or been in a fight. The little carer was born. Nothing was too much trouble in order to feel that, at least for a while, I was appreciated.

My operations on my ears continued until I was fifteen years, and my mother, valiant as ever to make me better, wrote to a well known hearing aid firm and asked for them to make a hidden hearing aid, following her design of a slide to go in my hair. I wonder, now, if she was the first to set the pattern for the behind-the -ear aids which followed later? Hers was such fierce love for me, and love that I have emulated for my own children.

Of course, as have many other deaf people, I have hidden my hearing aid from sight all throughout life. In the last five years, I have gradually trained myself to remove it most times, apart from when talking to some family members or people at work if there is no interpreter. Often I had trouble finding it, especially in the mornings getting ready for work. The reason for giving up on aids is because tinnitus and hypercusis make it hard to listen for long, together with speech discrimination problems. I am sure that there is scope for research into the long term effects of wearing hearing aids, but of course, those whose livelihoods depend on oralism will be reluctant to look too carefully into the negative aspects.

However, with regard to the need for spoken language development, I am eternally grateful for my mother's efforts, as she steered me from one ear, nose and throat consultant in my home town, to London and to the infamous Mr Ewing at Manchester. There I was looked after by Dot Miles, Deaf poet and actress, who was then an assistant at his clinic. She remembered me from all those years ago when we met just before she died so tragically. She too, was a victim of oralism. My mother was a fighter, and would not accept things if she believed otherwise. Without her I would not be who I am.

However, there is a sinister side to this, as the message that came home to me every day of my life, is the one that seeps into my soul: I was lesser than hearing people, no matter how hard I try to be equal. Without positive Deaf role models I was unable to feel I was equal. Rather than thinking of myself as a Deaf person I thought I was a stupid hearing person. With all the evidence set to show me this, struggling to obtain five O Levels, failing at Art College, being forced into work I never envisaged doing, and not having boyfriends, etc, all pointed to me being not terribly bright. My mother was unable to hide her shock at me passing the eleven plus, for it was obviously unexpected. My hearing brother was then doing his PhD at home, so the contrast between us was clear. Because I spoke so well and heard reasonably well in the small house we lived in, it was not really apparent to my family that I was as deaf as I am. Hearing people, and even some Deaf people, never understand this.

My philosophy to life became very fatalistic and hard on myself. I have poems I wrote which reflect that bitterness, that life was a long, up hill struggle which was to be endured and accepted quietly .One was about pilgrims and many about sacrifice. My mother used to describe me as "an earnest child". I think I was also a clever actress and this masked a deep depression which stayed with me, until recently.

The learning for self survival varies from one mainstreamed deaf child to another. Mine was to keep my head down (not difficult to do when you cannot understand the world about you) and to day dream. I hardly spoke but was constantly chastised when I did by teachers. I read all the time, making twice or three weekly visits to the library, reading books over again when I had read all in my age range, and starting on the classics by the age of nine or ten years old.

When I was at grammar school it became easier, because I was with girls who did not torment me in the same way as in the mixed infant and junior schools. We sat in rows with desks that had lids, and I would raise my lid (as if looking for a pen or paper) and gesture for assistance with page number or context of the lesson. I did make "friends" but we were always part of a gang, and with hindsight, I now see that they were all the working class girls from the docks. One left at fourteen years as she was pregnant. I missed her. I did not have any girls home from school until sixth form, and had only one girl I considered to be a friend at home, who went to a secondary modern school.

I remember very few names from school, especially not my teachers, and I look at my old school photo for recognition of an identity. I often never learnt their names in the first place. I remember those faces of girls who were kind to me; Lilian who wrote all the pop songs, would give me copies so that I could try to join in their singing at break times. I will never know if this was a conscious act or not, and

I certainly did not appreciate the deed at the time. No-one ever referred to me as having a hearing loss, except when I was in hospital again at eleven years old where my first form class sent me a letter hoping that I would be able to hear better afterwards. I certainly had no idea I was deaf then. I find it confusing: that on the one hand I hoped my hearing would improve as I knocked on the locker next to my bed after operations, but on the other to refuse to acknowledge that I had a hearing loss. If it was only so simple, I would have accepted my deafness straight away! We tend to put the blame on the individual for not accepting reality, and not the societal influences which cause the non-acceptance in the first place.

Being deaf was also a taboo subject at home. My mother proudly told my private hearing aid consultant that "I never talked about it", and I now realise that "it" meant being deaf. It was also the only time I recall deafness being mentioned until just before my father died fifteen years ago.

Even with my bone conduction hearing aid, I do not know how I managed at school, which was said to have given me good recruitment, so I must have heard more than many who currently attend mainstream schools. My hearing has since deteriorated, which puts me in a fair position to understand how deaf children struggle in their education. I know that hearing teachers can never understand what it is like to "cope". This is a word used constantly for deaf children in schools, and is seen as a means of helping us to deal with the adult hearing world, maybe to toughen us up? The other concept that disabled people have found is that of "triumph over tragedy" (T.O.T.) whereby the able bodied population applaud disabled people for breaking down barriers and achieving in the face of adversity. This may be well and fine, but to constantly jump over hurdles makes for exhaustion and "burn-out", and is not a realistic life expectation. Setting up deaf children for a life of TOT is harmful and unkind, although we need challenge and fighting spirit, it should not be excessive. Fun and recreation with other deaf people is essential for mental and physical health.

The coping mechanism that seems to be common amongst us DEXies, is the borrowed concept of "think-hearing identity." which DEX uses to explain what it is like for deaf people in deaf oral education, particularly those who are mainstreamed individually. This literally translates into "think-I-am-a-hearing person". I tried to sing, to act in school plays, to dance and to speak French and Latin, and to a certain extent, succeeded. I know hearing people will say "well done" and, of course, I take a certain pride in achieving. The principle, however, is that these acts were never done on the basis that I was a

Deaf person attempting to do hearing activities, but as another hearing person failing to keep up with other more able hearing people, and on the condition that I was as hearing as everyone else. The logical step, to me therefore, was if I was not achieving the same grades at my hearing peers, then I must be stupid. I started in top grades at grammar school and slowly worked down to bottom class in the fifth year, which is, common for deaf mainstreamed school children. If I had not had some "home tuition" from my older brother who was at university (but living at home,) then I would not have achieved as much as I did. These "tutorials " and help with home work were fraught with misconceptions as my brother struggled to reach my poor understanding, and build on it, but I simply did not have the background education on which to base his tutoring. Consequently he must have told my parents that I was not very bright. However, I now know that this is not really true, through counselling and a Deaf friend's support.

Labelling myself negatively and incorrectly has persuaded me that I was an unable, incompetent, uninteresting and wholly disposable person, and I have always suffered from a disabling shyness. There was a period in my life, during my twenties, when I would never use the word "I" and did everything in my power to avoid referring to myself at all in conversation. To a certain extent, this still stays with me even now.

This pattern has, naturally enough, brought on many life crises in adulthood. I have been married to two hearing men and seemed unable to make close or lasting friends, though I tried hard. I have had an abortion, and a still birth due to the debilitating tiredness I have had from depression and severe asthma, several suicide attempts and my first marriage was described by one doctor as "institutionalised rape". It was a short lived marriage of three years because my husband insisted on his marital rights every day and night: I had no understanding of sexual issues, and my husband took advantage of this. I also, as I have described earlier, needed to love too much, and was afraid of losing him if I did not grant sexual favours. It was a form of blackmail, and a sophisticated version of giving sweets out as I did at school. There were no children by this marriage although I had a termination before our wedding, as he was the father of the baby. I became pregnant through a complete lack of knowledge of conception and sex, even though I was twenty one years old at the time.

My second husband was my knight in shining armour because he had saved me from my first marriage. We were wed just ten months after I left my first husband, again because I was afraid to lose him.

All went well for the first few years. Cracks began to appear as life crises happened to us, but whereas most marriages can survive them, we did not have the essentials to weather the storms, despite our love. In my late twenties, asthma began. Then I felt flu-like all the time, and every task was an effort. I now know that it was the combination of Treacher Collins Syndrome and asthma/ allergies, which, unless carefully treated, produces symptoms not unlike M.E. My husband began to withdraw more and more into reading and listening to the radio. He was an active and loving father when my daughter and son were small but communication became more infrequent.

This resulted in my becoming even closer to my children and working even harder than before (I have always been a workaholic) even though I was tired all the time. I saw my G.P. who did not diagnose what I thought was M.E. so I had no medical support.

Several years later I stumbled upon an allergy specialist, which then set off eating problems as she put me on special diets. I became anorexic, and weighed six stones,(my normal weight is nine) as I was afraid to eat in case I reacted to certain foods, but with hindsight I had the classic symptoms of anorexia. Panic attacks had been a constant scourge throughout my life, but at this stage I had more severe breathing attacks where I could not use the shower or take baths.

There was absolutely nowhere I could not run and I felt trapped with nowhere to turn. During panic attacks I would self harm, hitting and banging my head on the wall or any other hard surface. Fortunately, I did not have enough strength to do any serious damage, but my hands and head hurt, as was my intention. I wanted to kill myself, but with two young children and a husband who professed to love me, I knew my family would be devastated. If I left them the same would happen and I did not know if I could live with my guilt feelings, having already once been divorced. Life presented no hope or joy at all. I simply did not want to live any more. Tired of putting a face to the world that did not reflect my feelings, I was exhausted with the sheer burden of tiredness and depression.

I drove to a local reservoir time after time, fully intending to jump in or to wade out to the deep waters. Drowning appeared to be a wonderful, slow release, a sleep-inducing way to die, immersed in the water I love so much. But each time I was tortured by the fact that I loved my children and my husband more than my death. I gazed out at the calming waters and took some energy from the beauty to sustain me instead, and this did help a little.

Over time, I made several pleas for help from my doctor and local psychiatric services. Twice I was referred to a psychiatrist, and twice community psychiatric nurses visited. Twice I drove, in a panic, to the accident and emergency clinic, but I was never admitted or referred for treatment to out-patients from there. I will never know if they did not care, or could see that it was reactive depression. I still have paranoid tendencies, where I feel that I am odd or people can see more of me than I know of myself. My sheer and utter morbidity and my desperation are only known to me, and can never be described with any satisfaction here. Those days and nights were an endless drudgery, for many nights I did not sleep well. The only relief I had were my children for I did all I could to hide my feelings from them: in fact they say that their childhood was good. As they became teenagers, though, they started to stay out more and more, as teenagers do, but I am sure, in part because of the depressed atmosphere in the house. My husband did not hide his depression so well. As said before, maybe I learnt very young to repress my feelings.

Finally, I started to fully appreciate and accept that it was by communicating through sign language that I felt free to express myself even though I think naturally in spoken language. There is no tension or tiredness as there is when lipreading or listening and talking. I craved to live with people with whom I could sign, and with whom I could feel truly supported. My Deaf identity began to emerge. I suppose this has been a life-time's work. Maybe it has always been there? The threads of my life have led to it.

From the time at Art College, where I could not understand the bearded tutors and decided to become a teacher of deaf children, to when I was taken on as an assistant teacher at the School for Deaf children and then referred on to the Principal Officer of the Society for Deaf People when I tried to gesture to the deaf children. (I knew nothing about the sign v oral debate, or any sign language, but gesture came naturally.) From there I got involved in work with Deaf people.

I subsequently met my first Deaf adult when I was nineteen years old, even though an older profoundly Deaf girl lived in my street. Much later she told me that when she was a child, intrigued by my massive box hearing aid, she had called several times to play with me, but my mother had said that I was not playing out. My mother never told me of this. I met the Deaf neighbour again a few years ago at a Deaf rally, and you can imagine how my Deaf ex- street mate and I emotionally cried and hugged each other when we worked out that her signing had resulted in us never becoming friends.

Working in the Deaf community was the greatest influence on my thinking. I discovered that deaf mainstreamed children were receiving fragmented services, or none at all. Some were signing, more had communication support and were in units with other deaf children. The majority are still not getting any support, like me. Deaf mainstreamed children were still being emotionally abused.

I began to put the pieces together and to see the parallels in my life. Over time I learnt a great deal about myself and about the system that had shaped us, and through this slow dawning of consciousness, lay the road to recovery. All the time I was Deaf but no-one had taught me what this meant. I found out by my work what I had been missing from Deaf culture. My social life centred around my family and a few hearing friends. I had been told not to mix with Deaf men as a young woman because of my work, and as a result, never met any Deaf man with whom I could share my interests. Although I did attend local Deaf functions as part of work, I never really socialised with Deaf people.

However, it was when I started to work with Deaf professionals that I realised that I was being labelled "oral" and "not really Deaf". It was painful to know that I was not being accepted amongst my own kind. It seemed the utmost cruelty to have been indoctrinated with the fact that I was a think-hearing person on the one hand by hearing people, and then again not to be allowed to be Deaf by Deaf people.

Really, deaf people have to pay for our pleasures, because of course life has to go on despite the daily slog of watching and listening through hearing aids: a life-time sentence in the hearing world, without remission, because of course, like all deaf people I had to think on my feet, expecting what hearing people are going to say, concentrating all the time to hear and lip-read and follow contextual and bodily clues. It is physically draining and exhausting, for me, resulting in tension pains in neck and shoulders. My G.P. has recently informed me that I have Repetitive Sprain Injury in my neck from the tension of lipreading and listening via hearing aids. In addition I have tinnitus and used to have hypercusis (sensitive hearing to certain frequencies,) but I don't have the latter now because I hardly ever wear my hearing aid.

It seems very unfair that deaf people cannot sign and relax within the Deaf community, knowing that we are accepted, and part of our group identity. At the same time I do not condone Deaf people's hostility to oral deaf people, because of their oppression by oralists. It is backlash. With information, many Deaf people are supportive of deaf ex-mainstreamers.

Simultaneously, during this awareness of Deaf people's attitude, my own self awareness was still being pieced itself together. A Deaf friend encouraged me to go for counselling, which lasted for about one year and this gave me the confidence to be assertive about my communication needs. It also helped me tremendously to work through my identity crisis. Also, my involvement with the Deaf Ex-Mainstreamers' Group offered so much mutual support that it was, literally, a life saver for me.

The counselling sessions also coincided with my second marital break-up. I suspect that the toll of my illness and deafness meant that my husband considered me to be too demanding with respect to my requests for clearer communication. He was naturally angry and upset. He could not understand why I suddenly needed to use BSL, but at the same time has worried about communication when family and friends were gathered together. Although my ex-husband has been to sign language classes he never picked it up as a second language because of lack of exposure and also relying on my speech, which always throws people off track, without consideration of the difficulties we have with receptive spoken language! I left after twenty two years of marriage.

Then, out of the blue, when I least expected it, I met a Deaf man; one of at least six generations of Deaf people, and a positive role model if I ever met one. Despite being from a Deaf family, he knew me and totally accepted who I am. He has changed my life for the better. There is no question about it now, that I am happier than I have ever been all my life, despite the usual problems that life challenges us all with. I compare the hearing world with the Deaf world, and know the need for both. I believe I am still on the fringe of Deaf culture, but I am more accepting of this, as it is at least far better than being alone on the fringe of hearing society. I am sure that I am seen as tougher than I am to hide the times without number when my confidence has to be nursed and my self esteem is rocky, but I have learned how to talk to myself and urge myself on. What more is there to say about this happier ending? Not walking into the sunset, but certain that I have seen a beautiful sun rise, and a closure on the grim past.

No deaf child should experience the childhood that deaf ex-main-streamers have. I know that some readers may think that we are, perhaps, full of pathos, sorry for ourselves, but I am known now for being a bit of a fighter. Maybe that was what it took to make me who I am?

But, personality issues aside, I am aware now that I am not a mirror to hearing people, and neither am I Deaf. At the same time, I have the same right to be Deaf as any Deaf person, and though the time was wrong for me and my deaf mainstreamed peers, I fervently hope one day all deaf children will be Deaf. I am sure that there is no need to put any child through hell to make her or him toughen up. The most important lessons in life are learnt through kindness as well as mistakes. It should be the child's mistakes, and not society's. And if the reader wonders why deaf children should be singled out for better treatment, against those who are abused in more obvious ways, then they need to consider what it must be like to be abused in any way.

Being normalised is in itself a form of abuse, no worse or less than any other kind because it forces deaf children to be normal, when it is clear that we are not "normal", for there is no such thing. All humans are different and unique, so all children, including deaf children, must be respected for who they are. To be Deaf is a gift which must be valued as much as life itself.

I hope that this account will at least make others aware of the dreadful deed of mainstreaming deaf children in its current form. Our truth is simple and true, and it is time for us to act.

Anon
February 2000.

15   *Letter sent to DEX*

Dear Dex,

I saw the programme today about the Deaf Ex-Mainstreamers Group, on Deaf World. I thought I'd write in as I am a deaf ex-mainstreamer too, and the comments on the programme brought back to me my experiences at school. I'm 18 years old and am re-sitting two of my A-levels as I want to go to university to study medicine, and I honestly feel that my situation will improve then (when I'm at university). I am the only deaf person in my family – I had meningitis when I was 4 years old – and as some other people in the programme felt, I think of myself as hearing, and always have. My problems started when I left primary school (which had a partial hearing unit and several other deaf people) and went to a public school on an Assisted Places Scheme at the age of eleven. Perhaps it was because I lost contact with the Deaf world and so did not know anyone who could understand my situation. I had some bad experiences during my early teens and lost all my confidence, and have only recently started to regain it. I am sure that my psychological health and my social life would not have suffered so much if I had known personally another deaf person in my situation.

Now that I have heard of the Deaf Ex-Mainstreamers Group, I know that there are other deaf people out there who speak like hearing people and had similar experiences to me at school. What I would really like though, is to meet people my own age who are like myself. I have tried the Deaf club, but I am not seen as "Deaf" because I am "different" – I don't sign and I have learnt to survive in the hearing world. I'm not seen as "hearing" either – when people find out I'm deaf, they treat me differently, sometimes even stop talking to me, as if I don't want to know their gossip! So I usually don't tell them, but this can cause problems if telephone numbers are exchanged and I forget to mention that I can't use the phone.

16   *"I put a lass in the bin, I do not know why."*

We lived in East Herringthorpe for six months. My little bastard of a brother kept getting into trouble so we moved back to Maltby to keep him on the straight and narrow, it did not work. He's still getting into trouble. When we moved back, I went back to St Mary's where I got into trouble again. I got sent out for something I can't remember what for now.

Anyway I'm now 5 and life seemed to be getting better (not!!). My brother (little bastard) got in trouble with the Police for first time when he was 3 for stealing from my mother. We'd been back in Maltby for about a year when one day someone dared me to stick a rubber up my nose, so I did. That afternoon I was taken to hospital to have the rubber removed.

It came to the summer. My dad took me, my older sister and my little twat of a brother on holiday. What a week. My dad and us lot went for a walk on the beach, I got soaked after falling in a giant puddle. My dad gave me his shirt to wear till we got back to the chalet we were stopping in. When we reached the top of beach this man, who had seen me fall in the puddle, gave me 50 pence. My dad took it off me for the electricity meter, I didn't get it back (skinflint!!!!). When we went back home and my parents started arguing, I went to the bedroom. I could not stand it when they argued.

A couple of weeks later we found out that I was deaf, my life has never been the same since. Always in hospital for operations on my ears. When I was in Infants 2, I still could not read, write or spell. I felt down because the lads could do something I couldn't. This gave me low self esteem.

In Junior 1 I always had to sit at the front of the class it wasn't fair. I hated wearing my hearing aid so sometimes I'd leave it at home, but I'd get done for not wearing it.

In Junior 3 I got told off for laughing in class and got sent out. In Junior 4 I had trouble with my spelling, so I spent half a day at a learning difficulties unit. I was at Listerdale for about six months, my reading and spelling improved but my writing and grammar still needed work.

A couple of months later I moved up to secondary school this is when life for me began to get unbearable, the lads kept calling me names and mocking me , so after some time I thought 'I don't have to put up with this'. So I started fighting back, the first time I grabbed hold of him and pushed him as hard as I could. He nearly went through the window on the second floor.

They left me alone for awhile , but it started again, so I told someone. But it only stopped for a few days then it started again I couldn't take it any more. It was making my life a living hell.

The next 3 years past slowly what with the name calling, course work and the arguments at home. In my 3rd year I took to taking painkillers just for the sake of taking something, I knew it would most probably cause me problems later on in life, but I didn't care. I just wanted to die. In my 5th year I was so sick of life so I took to taking blow.

My mother never found out that when I used to go to school I was mostly off my head. Things got worse and I started starving myself. One day I collapsed and that's when they all knew something wasn't right, so they sent me home.

A couple of months into my last year of school I started wagging lessons and going down town, just for some peace. Two weeks before my exams, this lad started on me so I got him by the neck and pushed him up against a wall, and just looked at him then I let him go. He went straight to the headmistress's office and told her exactly what I'd done, she came looking for me and gave me the third degree, so of course I wasn't taking it. So I told her "What do you expect me to do. stand there and take it" She replied "No, come and tell us". I just laughed and said "Every time I tell you they keep coming back for more". Anyway I was made to apologise.

The day my exams started things couldn't at the time get any worse because every time I sat an exam I felt sick. I didn't do too bad on my exams but could have done better.

When I left school the arguments at home were still going on. During the holiday I got a voluntary job in the British Heart Foundation shop, I liked working there, meeting new people and learning a trade. It was great.

Summer was over fast and I started college. On my first day it was scary I got lost and was late for a lesson. By this time I'd given blow the push and in January of my fresher year at college I started smoking because of the arguments and the work load.

The arguments at home started getting to me, then the work load because I couldn't concentrate at home, always wondering what the next argument was going to be about.

The first time I saw Maureen on a one to one basis was after I'd cracked a wall with my fist. She told me off and told me I should have spoken to someone. Life went down hill after that me and my mum's boyfriend nearly always arguing. Once I slept on the streets because I was too frightened to go home, so fed up of arguments and fights.

We had a person come to talk to us about drugs, I hardly said anything because I knew what drugs did to you. I started taking them. A few weeks later and things started looking up, (or so I thought), but things got worse. I made a big mistake one Christmas and I became pregnant. It wasn't my boyfriend's, when he found out he dropped me, but we made up a couple of days later. Then I found out he was cheating on me , so I got hold of him and asked him if it was true. He didn't answer so I got hold of the slag who was knocking him off behind my back and asked her. She said it was David (my boyfriend's name). So I slapped her and told him it was over. The day before Valentines, we were both miserable so my friend Vanessa got us back together.

He left college to go to Millside , so I left to spend more time with him. He did catering and I took up and been a care assistant for the elderly, so we only got to see each other every couple of days. I didn't like what I was doing at Millside so I left and went back to college.

I took up health and social care full time. Sometimes I wish I hadn't gone back. Since going back to college, I've battered walls and tried slitting my wrist, but it hasn't worked because I'm still here.

Life's a bitch and then you die.

Sherie Gibbons
1999

17 *Deaf community care?*

Presentation given at ADSUP seminar
(Association of Deaf Users and Providers) 1996

BACKGROUND ISSUES

"A Service on the Edge" S.S.I. Report concentrates on two groups of deaf people and is a timely and crucial inspection of very uneven or often poor service provision. Older deafened people who have lost their hearing identities need support in maintaining this whilst obtaining a more positive view of their new identity. Their needs are different from congenitally or early deafened children and adults who should be enculturalised biculturally or bilingually in order to become positive Deaf people and consequently are able to move flexibly as possible between hearing and Deaf cultures.

Normalised deaf people are those "who do not see themselves as part of the Deaf community", but the definition should not end there for us. "A Service on the Edge" recognises the need for a standard benchmark for individual assessments, care plans and quality service delivery of technical aids, information, advocacy, interpreting, consultation with deaf users, etc. There is, however, very little in it that addresses the demise of the Deaf community, and how that will impact on future generations of deaf children and even upon deafened older people who benefit from the norms and values of that culture. These values teach Deaf people to "think Deaf".

I believe we are watching the death of our community and its language. If it was a tribal language there would no doubt be an uproar in academic circles, with despair from those whose forbearers used them but only passing interest from imperialist language users whose language has granted them power. Approximately 98 per cent of world languages die and very few new ones are born to replace them.

Deaf people need a community and a fluent and spontaneous language, and because of the nature of our disability, cannot afford to lose it. Language and culture are inseparable. We Deaf people need a culture and a language that is our own, in order to affirm our deafness. This is integral to the development of Deaf identity.

94

Mainstreamed deaf children are denied access to their culture and language, but worst of all denied the ability to be themselves. David Dalby, Director of Observatoire Linguistique, says, "Language is a means of personal and group identity". It is interesting to note that many mainstreamed deaf children are high achievers academically, and so have a reasonable standard in written and spoken English. They are monolingual and even those who are proficient in English, once they learn BSL it becomes their preferred yet not fluent language.

Yet the professionals who once safeguarded, to a large extent, the Deaf way, are a derided profession of missionaries and welfare officers. They were patronising but they did serve a useful purpose in ensuring deaf communities developed and thrived. This does not condone the methods used to make deaf people dependent on them, but in changing the course of history by demolishing their roles, we have left a void. The new role of Deaf Community Development Worker is essential for the facilitation of community services.

In my dual roles as chair of the Deaf Ex-Mainstreamers' Group and as a manager of service for sensory disabled people in Rotherham, my employers have asked me to sign in a personal capacity. Social care legislation has not provided any guidelines which can incorporate a model of Deaf community care and, therefore, they are unable to veto DEX's views.

The future for congenitally deaf and early deafened people is bleak if we, as professionals working with deaf people, continue to ignore the facts. We know that Deaf clubs are closing or shrinking fast in attendance rates, particularly in rural areas. Some would argue that this is a sign that deaf people are becoming more independent so only a small core group require multi-service provision. Interpreting support as a single service is the growing norm. More and more Deaf people are becoming professionals, which means Deaf leaders are leaving their local communities.

The Deaf community is not being replaced by a new generation. Deaf divisions are perpetuated from an early age. From the day of diagnosis of deafness, or before if suspected, the whole machinery of oppression grinds into action. Deaf children are segregated because they are told they are not deaf enough for sign language, or too bright, or have oral skills, whatever that means. We are all too familiar with the dividing process that happens in education, but we stand by and do nothing.

The divisions, once established, are laid for life. Social Services still use the terms "deaf with speech", "deaf without speech", "hard of hearing" as specified by the Department of Health. Practitioners still regard sign language as being the prerogative of "profoundly Deaf" people. "Partially deaf" people are often viewed as being "not really deaf" and, therefore, do not really need social work intervention. Is deaf identity work widespread? Are workers with deaf people supporting deaf children, young people and adults in making the transition to becoming Deaf?

Social Services departments should play an essential role in the development of Deaf identities but as some local authorities have a child/adult service provider split, this makes it difficult for adult service providers to become involved with deaf children and families. The normalisation process that begins at diagnosis has to be prevented.

Out of a total of 693 establishments in the UK there are an alleged 55 which claim to be using a bilingual approach in the education of deaf children but only 12 of those are exclusively bilingual for all the deaf children in the school or unit (BATOD survey of 1996). The odds of deaf children belonging to the Deaf community at any stage in their lives is extremely low. DEX's findings are that "think-hearing" deaf people will most likely have:

– poor self images
– low confidence
– will have physical and mental health problems
– possibly be sublingual in spoken language, or linguistically delayed
– can be high functioning deaf people academically but socially inept
– or have poor general academic records.

The implications of the normalisation onslaught in education and in mainstream society has long lasting and traumatic results into adulthood. It is bound to affect future service provision in Social Services. The effects of normalisation calls for new skills in counselling on identity development and in Deaf community development so that "think-hearing" deaf people can have access to Deaf role models and a Deaf community in every local authority. The alternative scenario is that our profession of social workers with deaf people will go the way of our dying culture and language.

Resistance to social service intervention by "think-hearing" deaf people is a natural effect of normalisation. Why should deaf children and young people accept specialist services when they have been enculturalised as hearing people? This poses a grave problem for practitioners. Current legislation does not present a duty on local authorities to ensure a thriving Deaf community with its emphasis on individual assessments of need.

Deaf and disabled cultural needs are not incorporated into overall business plans. We need to be clear in defining deaf people's cultures as distinct from ethnic minority or indigenous hearing cultures, although obviously some Deaf people are multicultural.

Each culture must have its social and recreational activities. The National Assistance Act 1948 (29)(4)(f), and the Chronically Sick and Disabled Persons Act (2)(1)(c), calls upon all local authorities to provide social and leisure activities to disabled people. Joint Commissioning Teams (or panels, etc) and elected members of councils have the power to ensure that disabled peers groups can meet in welcoming surroundings. Community Care legislation has overtaken other disability legislation because supporting people in the hearing community is now fundamental to Social Services' survival with increasing cutbacks from central Government. The culture is to maintain in the community; for hearing people this is imperative: what about maintaining deaf people in our own community?

The Association of Directors of Social Services recent budget survey states that there will be average reductions of £2.5 million (3.88%) per authority in 1998/99. It notes that grants to voluntary organisations are commonly being cut or frozen (25%). "This often adversely affects the necessary community support networks."

Since many local authorities provide funding to voluntary association Deaf clubs or provide day centre facilities to deaf people for their social evenings, etc., they are the mainstay of the Deaf community's survival. It is imperative that funding and inflationary consideration continues.

Future of deaf community care

Standard Transitional Grants (S.T.G.) funding will elapse in 1998, and although ring-fenced budgets will discontinue, the regulations and contract arrangements will be service purchase led. This could mean that we can insist on community care for deaf people, in its real sense. S.T.G. funding cannot be relied upon to provide grants to voluntary organisations if they offer social or drop-in centres, but can fund information services, for example. One way round this stumbling block, for me, was to ask the local Deaf club committee to become service providers of an advice centre. With the removal of criteria we can now insist on community development.

What means are there to facilitate Deaf community care?

Dex's recommendations

1. A national educational policy for sign bilingual programmes to be implemented in each area in conjunction with education/health

and voluntary agencies. This is according to Deaf users' wishes and in light of our own experiences.

2. Families to be offered an intervention programme as part of a multi-agency package:
   - a Deaf befriender
   - sign language classes and involvement with the Deaf community in a safe environment
   - support networks of other parents
   - encouragement, advocacy and information at all stages by a key worker
   - support networks for their deaf child and strong deaf peer group.

3. Deaf service users to have access to a variety of social and leisure activities, and educational and vocational training in their own communities, whether it is for deafened (HOH) people or for BSL users.

4. Young non-BSL using adults and people to be supported in gaining a positive Deaf identity, either by individual care plans or in group work activities, i.e. Deaf youth work.

5. All professionals who work with deaf people should be trained in Deaf cultural awareness and its importance for individual deaf children and their families and its beneficial impact throughout their lives.

6. Deaf community development to thrive on the view of community members. The skill mix in each Social Service/voluntary organisation may need to be reviewed to incorporate the following posts:
   - Deaf Community Development Worker/Deaf Youth Worker
   - Advice Worker
   - Interpreting Service
   - Technical Officer
   - Social Worker with deaf people and/or assistant.

Deaf social care cannot remain a "Service from the Edge" and deserves appropriate capital expenditure to match clear gaps in service provision. The onus falls on Social Services to lead other agencies, a major responsibility that cannot be shirked. We need to work in partnership to stem the tide of normalisation which is the imposition of one language and one culture, and which is, basically, hearing imperialism: "Resistance, far from being merely a reaction to imperialism, is an alternative way of conceiving human history. It is particularly important to see how much this alternative preconception is based on breaking down the barriers between cultures," says Edward D. Said in "Culture and Imperialism". As mediators between cultures, and as practitioners working with deaf people, we are in a position to enculturalise deaf people and their families towards "think-Deaf" identities.

Yet at the same time practitioners working with deaf people have colluded in deaf disempowerment, in normalisation without realising, "by authors who lived with and within the policing strategies"... "What I am interested in are the strategies for breaking it" (Toni Morrison 1992). To conclude, we have the power to make our own history or Deaf-story.

Jill Jones

What do I do? Where do I go? I just don't understand.

3.45 is here again, almost like a daily sin, the depressions of the day have just worn in.

Everybody going on from every direction possible, after a while it starts to annoy me. Once annoyed I get upset. Sometimes I still don't feel that I belong in this world.

My parents and everyone around me can hear properly, why is it that I feel like I am travelling down a street with a dead end and there is no way out.

Of course I would never expect a hearing person to understand. I am not saying that they don't try, but I need to talk to someone who understands, but I know no one. So I talk to paper and write down what I often fear.

Things just get bottled up and every once in a while I just crack, all these fears, thoughts and feelings which I can't express to anyone close to me, so I just bottle them up until I crack! It is my way of dealing with life, perhaps not the best one after all!

What do I do? Where do I go? I just don't understand.

Charlotte Dixon (age 17 yrs.)
4:00pm 9/2/00

Letter to Dex

I have never met anyone in my entire life like myself who has been similar thing and communicates in the same way with much in common. That's very demoralising as you may know. As I understand, I think this group or organisation was set up to put people like me in touch with each other.

If you are not such a group could you please put me in touch with an organisation which specialises in this purpose. I would be extremely grateful if you could help in some way at least.

18 *To be or not to be mainstreamed*

1. Pre-mainstream stages

Mainstreaming in an ordinary school is something that I've experienced in the 1970s. This involved integrating with hearing peers and having no contact with deaf people at all. I was mainstreamed in two different schools, which were the primary and the secondary comprehensive from when I was 9 years old and did not leave until 15 years old.

Before the age of nine, I attended a local school for the Deaf for the first 5 years, which was in the latter part of the 1960s' and up to 1972. In that time, I interacted socially with other deaf children and communicated with them using sign language that was consistent with deaf people in Leicester. I've enjoyed the gibes, quips, banter, laughter and the odd gossips from time to time with the deaf peers. At the weekends, I frequented the local Deaf centre, which involved other deaf children from our school and further contacts with deaf adults whom were role models to us.

My mother used to take me to the local Deaf Centre, as she was a committee member for a time with the local deaf children's society. As we did not have a car at that time, therefore had to endure travelling, which involved two different means of public transport across the city. My parents obviously made many allowances for me to participate socially with other deaf peers at that time. As being working class, the source of income was that my father was a regional secretary for a local Trade Union and my mother was a clerical assistance in some factory. Although, both parents were quite educated and politically motivated by the Trade Unionist / Socialist movements, they followed professional advice from the school and the hearing impaired service about my upbringing. However, I've communicated orally with my family at home and never used sign language at all with them. Only my immediate family could understand me when I communicated orally. I was embarrassed using sign language outside the school and the Deaf Centre at the time and aign language was only to be used privately with deaf peers, away from the eyes of hearing people, as it was a taboo thing to do in front of hearing people. I remember quite well that when attempting to communicate orally with hearing children in my neighbourhood, they have had a big problem in understanding me and I, them.

2. Primary mainstream school

My time in the Deaf school was soon to end in 1972 and I transferred to an ordinary primary school at nine years old with one another deaf peer from the deaf school. We spent our next two years in the Partially Hearing Unit (PHU), which consisted of some ten other deaf pupils. I was quite shocked, when I went to the playground on the first day, as no one could socially interact with me and deaf children from the unit. Most of us from the unit stayed together as a group. This was the first time I realised the differences in the Deaf school and the ordinary school. There was minimal verbal teasing in which I did not realise these forms of 'them and us' pattern. Therefore, the deaf children from the unit have shown me the way to be cautious of myself of the differences between hearing and deaf peers.

Strangely enough, I was not aware that the 'them and us' pattern existed when I was with the hearing children in the neighbourhood before. After a few weeks of starting the primary school, my awareness had increased of the inability to communicate or to integrate socially with the hearing children in the neighbourhood. I felt limited in the social interaction in both the neighbourhood and the school and could only interact socially with those from the unit and the Deaf Centre. Over the next few weeks, we were quite close to one another for friendship and security where ever and when ever possible such as in the Unit and more so in the playground. If any of the deaf peers or I were threatened or in trouble by hearing peers then we would come in aid of each other with a feeling of 'tribal kinship'. This continued to do so throughout my time there.

The only time I was ever mainstreamed at that school was usually in physical education and Arts subjects, with hearing peers. The rest of the core and foundation subjects were taught by the Teacher of the Deaf, which was based in the unit and with other deaf peers. In that first year, in the formal mainstreamed setting, which was the classroom I paired up with another deaf peer, although he should have mixed with those in the year above me. The following year I was on my own in the mainstreamed classrooms that I attended with hearing peers, as he had left once he reached the mandatory secondary age to start at a deaf boarding school. I was quite upset at the loss of the deaf companion with whom we attended the mainstreamed classrooms together.

The importance for me to have the deaf companion was that I could enjoy the experience gibes, quips, banter and laughter. However, I felt lonely and did not interact at all with the hearing peers. I was happier in the unit as long as there was a sufficient number of deaf peers for me to interact socially. There were moments when we could enjoy lip-reading out to each other for gibes, quips, banter and laughter unlike in mainstreamed classrooms. The teacher of the deaf was excellent when teaching core and foundation subjects, but she told us from time to time never to use sign language in the classroom and the playground, because the hearing children would view us as 'being silly'.

However, this was to create the impetus for being oral and the beginning of neglecting the use of sign language. Furthermore, the deaf peers would play a game with each other to see who had the best speech and to prove that we could communicate with the hearing 'friends' in the playground and this was encouraged by the teacher. Another game that we played was that each of us would wear headphones, cover our mouths, say certain words to each other, and see if we could recognise such words. For us it was a good excuse for not doing any schoolwork and was happy to do this game. But, it was a catch-22 situation as for me, it was so frustrating although there were sounds to be heard from the headphones, but unintelligible. As far as I can remember, of the ten deaf pupils, three had poor speech and uses full sign language and the rest of us including me used sign language, but supported with the use of speech. Those games led us to try and 'out do' each other to see who was the best, but this led to severe consequences, which resulted in jealousy, having fights and bickering with each other. Somehow, we managed to continue to support each other in the face of hearing adversaries in the playground.

Coming to the end of my tenure at that primary school, questions were asked as to where they could send me – the deaf boarding school or a local comprehensive only two miles from my home. The parties involved in this discussion were my parents and the hearing-impaired service. About half the number of deaf children in the unit was about the same age as me and they too face the similar dilemma. My parents, by then had some awareness of my needs to mix more with deaf peers, they engaged in some campaigns to have me sent to a deaf school. Partly, because by then I understood the differences between the hearing and deaf school placements and supported the idea of going to a deaf school. The Hearing-Impaired Service for Leicestershire, as I learnt later, have had a policy of integrating deaf children to local hearing schools and be taught orally. The head of the Service as I remember had the last word and decided that it was best for me to be sent to a hearing school. I never learnt how the other deaf peers from the same primary school were sent to different deaf schools, therefore as far as I know I was the only one to be sent to a hearing secondary school because the school I was supposed to go to was too full.

3. Secondary school

Regarding further contacts with deaf peers, I learnt later from my parents that on the advice from the Head of Hearing-Impaired Service that it 'was in the best of interests for everybody' that I should cease contact with other deaf peers at the Deaf Centre. This was the aim of the hearing-impaired service in order for me to integrate in a wider field such as in the evening and weekends other than being main-streamed in the secondary school. However, my parents continued to take me into the Deaf centre's youth club and let me go on weekend trips with them in the summer holidays, but not as frequent as before. Over the period from leaving the primary school to leaving secondary school, my contact with the deaf world slowly dwindled, but I did not altogether lose contact.

The first year of my secondary comprehensive was worse as compared with the primary school. The teacher of the deaf was a lazy teacher. He was a youngish sporty type whose love for cricket and football, meant spending most of his time 'doing shadow-bowling' against a wall in the unit with a small bouncing ball (probably confis-cated from other pupils). I spent more time in the Partially Hearing Unit and most of the time on my own, although there were other deaf peers but they were of different ages and I was the only deaf in my year. Therefore, he only gave me the work on whatever topic is needed, such as English and Maths from the textbooks at the start and then left me to my own devices. The subjects that were given to me in the unit were in fact already learnt from the primary school age. Being alone in the unit made matters more difficult as I was used to interacting with deaf peers in classrooms and in the playground in the previous school, therefore missing the gibes, quips, banter and laughter terribly. This new pattern overnight forced me to spend some alternative arrange-ments for myself or 'shadow' the hearing peers in which I could not interact as well as I could to some extent in the previous school.

My time at the first year was influenced by the backdrop at the height of the troubles in Northern Ireland, which was in 1974. The school has a high percentage of Irish and Asian immigrants. There was frequent bullying of Asian children, but it was worse with Irish children, which was motivated by the news of IRA terror in Northern Ireland and other racial prejudices as well as anyone who looked and acted differently. Unfortunately, my deafness did not help to pacify the prejudices. For security, I mixed with the Irish, the Asians and sometimes with one older deaf peer (4 years older) rather than with English-white peers. When interacting with the immigrants, it was more 'hanging around' with them rather than conversing with them socially, they accepted me superficially. Nearly everyday, I was in fights at break times in either the playground, school corridors and in the playing field. The reason for those fights was because I had been subjected to failure to understand any hearing peers when they made attempts to communicate with me and I would ask them to repeat or whatever, but my responses were rebuked by laughter and mimicking of my speech. I have been nicknamed 'dummy', 'Deaf bastard', 'Here comes the Deaf twat', etc.

I tried to fit in the 'norms', the behaviour required for interaction with hearing peers as part of their 'code of conduct', which involved supporting the same football teams, popular pop music or even participating in delinquent matters. Although, I was never able to follow the results and the gibes of football I pretended to know it all from time to time just for the sake to be part of the group of hearing peers, because of the risk. There was at this particular time a fashion amongst the boys, when supporting a pop group like the 'Bay City Rollers', nearly everyone in the school was wearing tartan-lined trousers and jackets. Therefore, I continued wearing school uniform and did not follow the fashion trend of the Bay City Rollers. This was one of many examples of not following the 'code of conduct' of the time, which resulted in being teased, involved in fights or even rejection by the hearing peers.

Quite frequently, the fistfights and name calling extended to the mainstream classroom and on the way home at the end of each day. Eventually, I had to run the gauntlet in the fear of getting caught and bullied on the way home from school. This resulted in going home using different routes at that time which I am sure would be the envy of the local cartographers when plotting for ordnance survey maps of the area of Leicester. The fights continued in the playground and classrooms, but on the way home the problem dwindled as I had a bicycle, on which I could escape quickly.

In terms of travelling, whilst in both the deaf school and the primary school, I travelled by using minibuses, which was provided by the local council for deaf and blind children from home to schools in Leicester. However, that ended when I started the secondary school, yet some of the deaf children that I knew from the previous two schools still travel in the same school bus. In the secondary school, I used to wait at the main school gates at the end of the day to catch a glimpse of the deaf children in the bus and wave or communicate with them briefly, as the bus stopped to pick up other deaf pupils from the school. I did not stop there, as I was so keen to maintain contact with other deaf children.

At lunchtimes, during the first few months of starting the school, I sneaked out of school and crossed the road to meet with other deaf peers that I once knew who were still at the primary school. I went to converse with them through their school railings. The teachers of the deaf from both the schools found out and put a stop to that. It was not until the third year, when it was permissible to go out of school at lunchtimes, by then the deaf peers I knew from the primary school had already left. Instead, I went for walks in the nearby park or leafed through magazines in newsagents. If it wereas raining, I would go into the school library, which was usually closed at lunchtimes and read books, as the librarian seemed to be understanding of my predicament of mixing with hearing peers.

There were two Irish hearing peers that I befriended with from the First Year at the school, but the friendship was more superficial as compared with their friendship with other hearing peers themselves, especially when engaging the usual gibes, quips, banter, laughter and the odd gossips. My friendship was more based on non-verbal interaction, which involved in playing games in the playground at times. Those were ball games and quite often at other times when they engaged in conversation with other hearing peers, I stood in the background as a 'shadow' with such patience that I started to day dream.

One of them did invite me round to his house for tea from time to time, where his large family was very welcoming. This soon led to interaction with my family and forming a friendship which was to last a good few years. The Irish friend became deaf aware, but not fully, in the course of visiting the Deaf Youth Club and summer deaf holiday camps with me. He never learnt sign language, but used gestures and mime with other deaf children. Although, back at the school, he still left me out when he engaged conversation with hearing peers from time to time. I pressed on to find out what was being said only to be rebuked with 'I don't know; I'll tell you later' or 'Nothing, not important'. This continued right up to the Fifth year.

Mainstreaming in classrooms started from the first year, this began with Physical Education, Arts and Craft subjects, as in the primary school. The year structure of the school was spread out to cope with a part of over 1000 pupils of the whole school, with each year being divided to different groups. Each year was divided to those who did well were classed as 1A1 and those who were poor in subjects such as English and Maths were as 1C. When starting at the school, I was registered with 1C, which was the bottom of the year group! How the professionals determined my needs and put me in that group, I never found out. There was a time when the teacher of the deaf was ill for a couple of weeks and there was no teacher cover in the unit, so I was put into the 1C class, which consisted of some 20-30 pupils. In that class, the pupils were Asian, who spoke little English and there were some Irish children.

In those two weeks, in nearly all the subjects in which I participated, I came top of the class in textbook work, grammar and spelling. The children i my group had to grapple with very simple words and to work with the dictionary when required. As a year tutor discovered my talent, I was moved to 1B3 in the second term. Still, in that group I continued to be top of the class. The scope of mainstreaming increased in the Second year to cover more subjects, but I was still withdrawn from time to time to work in the unit. In the Second year, I was moved to 2B1 and the rest of the hearing peers, whom I shared with in 1B3, remained in 2B3, even though I was quite good with my subjects in that year and above average as compared with others in 2B1. There was some resentment amongst the 2B3 pupils caused by jealousy and they could not wait to seek me out at break times and to bully me. Over a period in that Second year, my work started to fail me through constant bickering and jeering in the classroom.

This was made worse, when I was supplied with a rudimentary radio aid, which was a large black box that rested next to my chair and the teacher wearing a huge microphone. The pupils would creep up behind me and tug out my hearing aid wire attached to my mould in the ear and this would cause feedback and whistling, therefore leading to embarrassment. The pupils who had done that would get off lightly as teachers sometimes shared the humour of it. The black box had a shoulder strap connected with it, which was heavy to carry, I was told to take good care of it and never let it out of my sight, which was a huge burden to have at break times. Eventually, I would find somewhere to hide it like in the bushes or the dustbins until I would need it.

Understanding teachers in mainstreamed classrooms in each subject varied; I had to rely 100% of the time on lip-reading, regardless of using my hearing aid support with the loop system provided by the microphone and black box. Most of the teachers talked many times and at times have had their back to the classroom when writing the blackboard or walking around the room and I would try to follow their lips whenever possible. Sometimes, they would talk continuously throughout the session and it was a huge strain of having to lip-read, therefore I would get very frustrated. Eventually, I would either day dream or try to copy the others' workbooks at the next desk and would face complaints from the pupils to the teacher. I would get a missile, such as a blackboard rubber or chalk, thrown at me by the teachers or even a slap on the back of my head, because of complaints. The black box was never a good help, as some teachers refused to wear it anyway. I stopped wearing it when I reached half way into my fourth year, as I was confident enough to challenge the teachers and know when to say no. As far as I can remember the teacher of the deaf in the unit would complain nearly every time that I was not paying attention. He informed me that the teachers came up to him in the staff room from time to time to make a complaint about me. The fact was that he was aggrieved that he had to endure the battery of complaints when he wanted to relax in the staff room!

Throughout the period of five years, my work was of high standard at the beginning and faltered toward the end. This was the culmination of failure to interact in teamwork, in which I remember having lower marks than anyone else was and failure to understand instructions through the impatience of the teachers. The greater factor was probably due to bullying and my understanding of classroom instructions given out was based on a lot of guesswork. I was probably indebted to the primary school teacher of the deaf for the high standard of teaching which prepared me for the secondary school. However, I was disappointed in the capacity of the secondary school and the role played by the unit in its failure to maintain a standard of education, lacking deaf awareness by the staff and its failure to take any preventive action.

In the first two years of that school, when in mainstreamed classroom, I have had experience of pairing up with hearing peers, but not to a great extent in comparison to other hearing peers working with each other. Even when forced by the class teacher, the pupils with whom I would be sitting or working with would retort to protest.

In the first year, especially in the 1B3 class, for a short time I shared a desk with one girl who was helpful in letting me look at her work from time to time when I could not understand the teachers. She was left out in social interaction as she was the fattest in the class, but she was bullied continually by others when we sat together on one desk. She stopped working with me, as she was teased on sexual references by sharing the desk with me. At another time, I managed to work with one pupil in the second year only because I had the best set of multi-coloured pens he would 'scrounge' from time to time. He moved off once the pens were worn out to be with another pupil.

The third year I was at my zenith and continued like this right to the end of my fifth year in being teased and getting involved in punch fights. I was in the class of 3B1, which had the same pupils from the 2B1 of the previous year. The problem of bullying and fights carried over to the third year by the same group. This was when the form teacher and the teacher of the deaf became aware of the problems I was facing. I was given an option by a year teacher to move from 3B1 to 3B2 and I refused. The reason for that refusal was that it has taken me two years to move up from 1C to 3B1 and I did not intend to step backwards and join a class of under-educated pupils. Perhaps, if the option were the other way to 3A3 then I would have accepted. Therefore, I remained with the 3B1 and had to endure the battle. The awareness remained amongst the teachers of the problems that I had in my third year, so I was moved to a different class in the fourth year to 4A4. However, the problem worsened in the playground, but to some extent there was an improvement with the new class, although there were still teasing about my deafness, albeit to a lesser extent. At that point, at the beginning of my fourth year, I learnt to stop making complaints as this would make the bullying worse. That was when, I assume, the teachers believed that things were getting better for me, I even lied from time to time just to protect the others.

From the fourth to the fifth year, I stayed on with the same class, but still there were no respect from the hearing peers. Half way through the fourth year, the problems increased with the class and continued throughout the fifth year. By then I was a 'nerd' of the school.

There was this particular day in April that hardened my position with that school. On that same morning, I had three fights: one in the corridor of the school at break times; another in the school's common room for fifth years, resulting in a broken window; and with a deaf peer. This time, after facing the year teacher, I was told to be expecting a detention, but I ignored him and left school on the spot, only to return for my final CSE exams, two weeks later.

The CSE exam period was an interesting one. Everyone was given pre-exam techniques a few weeks before and given support for revision. I was taken out of the mainstream classrooms and was given similar support from the teacher of the deaf in the unit. The length of time given to me to make preparations was less than the others in their own classrooms as I did not participate with them, as they were working in teams testing each other for knowledge. English language was one of the exams that I took and it was divided into three parts. The first part was oral discussion with an external examiner face to face, and I had a rough time trying to lip-read the person. This was meant to last 20-30 minutes, but I stayed for 10 minutes.

The second part of the English exam was English Comprehension, which involved listening to the tape and me being given a list of questions on a paper. This was due to take place in a classroom with 30 pupils who were listening and writing down the answers, but I did the exam in the unit with the teacher of the deaf acting as invigilator. I did not understand a word that was being said from the tape, therefore a lot of guesswork was involved by looking at the questions and imagining the answers. The third part was the English Composition, which involved writing a story along with others in a main hall and the exam time was the same for me as those with the hearing peers. The CSE exam result for English came out as graded four, which was one of the lowest and one step away to failure.

My view of sport is a poor one, as this possibly reflected to my involvement in the Games and Physical Education at the secondary school. I used to love sport, such as football, rugby, tennis and any team sport. This stemmed from the sporting activities at the deaf school and to a lesser extent in the primary school. In my opinion, I was quite good at playing football. The positive view of team sport was soon to change sometime in the first few months of starting the secondary school. All of the first years from different class groups participated every weekly afternoon and they would have a choice in either football or rugby, which I would choose in turn weekly.

My enthusiasm turned sour for a number of reasons. One of those was that every time we had a team selection motivated by a popular pupil or favouritism made by the pupils I would be selected last or not at all, until forced to do so by the teacher on the spot. The other reason, in the course of the game not one person would pass me the ball or there was a good chance of getting fouled or kicked.

Therefore, every time the Games session come on, I would make all kind of excuses to get out of it, such as being sick or having a bad leg. That would result in the punishment of either copying word for word from a school hymnbook or slaps with a plimsoll by the PE teacher across my thighs, if a sick note not produced. Over the period, I would choose to participate in 'individual sport', which was playing tennis against a wall or Ping-Pong with another hearing peer. Today, I still view competitive sport with distaste, as a result of lacking involvement in the PE teams in the school.

My relationship with deaf people from when I started at the secondary school to my 20s' dwindled quite rapidly. Although, my relationship with those from the unit at the primary school was good at that time, my attitude changed over the period and I viewed the deaf people as mere inferiors. I felt superior compared to them at the local deaf centre, as I could communicate with hearing better than the 'lot of them'. I viewed myself as different from them and not like them at all. I even labelled myself as partially hearing and hated the word 'Deaf', therefore growing my hair to cover my hearing aids to hide my deafness. Even at school, I regarded the other deaf pupils from the unit as inferiors.

This was the result of being told to drop using sign language by both the teachers of the deaf from the primary and secondary schools. I lost the use of sign language at 12 years old and had even forgotten the art of finger spelling. At the Deaf Centre, I used to show-off my skills of being 'oral' and teased the deaf peers for not being able to speak and being a bunch of 'dumb' idiots. This has created enmity toward me by the deaf peers there, and it resulted in having being bullied and to endure fights over the period. I still felt however, a sense of belonging with the deaf people as compared with the hearing counterparts from the school. I could still communicate them, despite the fact that I 'lost' my signing skills, so I resorted to lip-reading them aided with 'rough' gestures. During relationships with the deaf people at that time, I lost the art of the gibes, quips, and banter and especially of all the laughter.

My home life during the Secondary school years was full of frustration in the evening and weekends. I used to come home from school feeling frustrated and upset at times, although the only person I could have a laugh and the odd gossip with was with my mother, as I could not form social interaction with anyone else. There were attempts made by my parents to improve my 'listening skills' such as communicating on the telephone and buying me talking tapes for me to listen.

There was one occasion, I was given headphones, a tape and a book, both called the 'Guns of Naverone', written by Alistair Maclean. I was supposed to have had listened to the words flowing through from the tape recorder and read word for word from the book, but this was a huge strain. From time to time, I would give up and refused to do it any more, but my parents forced me to do this most times. I used to have tantrums and fights with every member of my family sometimes. For relaxation, I used to watch a lot of the pre-teletexted television in those days and disappear on a bicycle over a long period to escape the pressures of tantrums at home.

Looking back now, I realised that as far as social interaction in the school was concerned it was with the Asian and Irish pupils, as explained earlier. In the later stages of the school, girls were friendlier to me than males. It was only in the Fifth year that I managed to share the same desk with an Irish girl. She was more understanding of my situation compared with anyone else I had been in contact with in the school in that five years.

It was through her that I developed a taste for motorcycles when she invited me round to her house party one Saturday evening. In that party, I was surprised that the people did not come from the school, but were local bikers, hippies and punks with fantastic colourful hair-styles and compared to anyone from the school those people were friendlier and understandable to my needs. Since walking out of the school, I have had not been in contact with the pupils at all, apart from those two Irish pupils, for a short while, that I mentioned earlier.

In my fifth year, we had a series of career visits to the school from different companies readily to employ school leavers for apprentice-ships. One of them was a visit from the British Army. That day, the Army visit to the school had provided an impressive array of displays out on the school field, which tempted me to join the Army. I was so naïve about my deafness at the time that I decided to follow hearing peers on once I left the school. Unsurprisingly, I was turned down because of my deafness and I understood it and accepted my limitation there.

4. Post-school era

By 1979, since leaving the secondary school and gaining qualifications of six out of seven CSEs with low grades, I enrolled at a Sixth Form College in the hope of gaining O Levels and eventually A Levels. The atmosphere at the college was much better, but social interaction with the hearing peers was superficial, as I could not enjoy the gibes, quips, banter and the gossips with them. The interaction was more small talk routines, although they welcomed me into their groups at breaktimes, only for short periods until they got bored with me. As there was a 'time limit' of between a few days to a few months for hanging around with any group, I used to seek out different groups to join from time to time. I never was able to follow the banter with anyone and even with deaf people themselves. My relationship with deaf people was more or less superficial in my teenage years.

In 1979, at 16 years old, my first ever outing with a group of Deaf adults came with a shock. I went on a day trip to Blackpool Deaf Rally with a group of deaf people from Leicester Deaf Social Club. I was shocked, as my concept of the amount of money needed to spend as an adult compared to the smaller amount of money that I bought with me was different. They knew the management of spending power which I lacked. I still had the concept of spending money confined to sweets and comics, with enough for fish and chips. The realisation dawned on me the difference between being a youngster and that of being an adult. This outcome resulted in derisory laughter from everyone on the coach trip.

The technique of gibes, quips, banter as used by anyone as part of the behaviour that is required for social interaction did not work at all for me with the hearing peers at the secondary school and then after. This extended with deaf people in general and was at some point lower than when I was eleven years old. I had a problem in forming a conversation with anyone, as I did not know how to have the 'knack' for developing a conversation. I managed to learn slowly how to ask questions and make small talk with both deaf and hearing people, since leaving school.

In that period as a teenager, I was so desperate for friendship with people that I spent more time taking the 'hedonist' approach than doing my college studies. I went to parties, night outs in the town and heavy rock night-clubs, at frequent times on my own. I used to 'hang-about' with a bunch of delinquents such as bikers, hippies in pubs and motorcycle rallies. I had a fiery temper, which at times went out of control. I was involved in fights, for two reasons, such as the result of deaf discrimination from the hearing to supporting 'friends' who were already involved in fights of their own making. I finally gained respect from those people when I bought my first motorcycle.

The purpose of having the motorcycle for me was to have a sense of belonging and a feeling of 'camaraderie' with the social group that existed at the time.

I learnt a trade at a college for three years, learning commercial photography, but the outcome had devastating results that would force me to give up the trade. I was shortlisted for a job interview as one of two people with the Leicestershire Constabulary Forensics Department. The job was given to the second person, because I could not use a police radio!

That was a huge feeling of let down at this point. I resented myself as a deaf person. I did freelance for a time with various newspapers and motorcycle journals for two years, but the discriminatory attitude of the other photographers and journalists made my work harder, so I was forced to give it up when not making enough money out of it. Since then, I had developed a fear of working for hearing people, because of their discriminatory attitudes toward me which never enabled me to be part of the workforce.

From 1984, my sign language skills improved when by chance I was given a job working with a workers' co-operative printing press company ran by a group of deaf people in London. My attitude towards deaf people had remained the same as I was in the secondary school. This caused some resentment among the deaf workers toward me, but some of them were patient enough with me to a certain extent. I stayed there for nearly five years. During that time, I went to

London College of Printing in Elephant and Castle for three years as part of day release apprenticeship. I had a rough time there, because of discriminatory attitudes from the hearing students and I was lonely.

The first year in London was rough, as I did not have any friends at all. I frequented pubs every night in West London on my own. I managed to join the Acton Deaf Club, but could not fit in with any of the deaf people there. The best break for me was that I joined the 66 Club in the West End and found there were similar 'oral speaking' and SSE signing deaf people there. I managed to get respect from them better than from the deaf people at Leicester, but only superficially. My problem was worsened by the fact that I turned up riding a motor-cycle, wearing oily jeans complete with bike leathers, and sporting a beard, which did not help to allay fears. My image as a biker probably has ruined my moments with the deaf people in London and there were fruitless attempts to find other deaf bikers. The biker image comes complete with riding rumbling British-made motorcycles and wearing 'tatty' looking open faced helmets was a hearing made sub-culture and finding a similar deaf equivalent was harder than I thought it would be. I turned to those bikers in hearing world for camaraderie. It was hard shedding off the 'biker-image', as by then I was involved in the bike world for 6 years. By then, my liking for riding motorbikes was strengthened by the fact that it was useful for getting around in London, for speed and easy to park.

I worked in two more different printing companies run by worker co-operatives. Although I had attitude problems with the former deaf workers, I had a greater problem with the hearing workers in those two different co-operatives. The first company, I lied through the teeth to get a job there. I told the interviewer, when quizzed about my deaf-ness that I could hear most things, when in reality I could not. The first few months was just settling in and getting to know the people and the place, I was happy for a time.

Things started to change when I could not hear the instructions about certain jobs from time to time, and I thought I understood what was being said, so I ended up getting some tasks wrong at great financial cost to the company. The other problem was that I could not get involved in gibes, quips, and banter with the hearing staff. Therefore, this affected my relationship with the other workers and this led me to lose my motivation, confidence, and end up with not concentrating on my job properly leading to further mistakes. I was there for 15 months, in which time half of the workforce were given redundancy and I went with it. In another job with a printing co-operative I was more laid back than in the one I was made redundant from. But, there was a completely different problem, as the negative attitude of deaf people did not help my position there. My job was to upgrade the department, technically, but they were not too keen in having a deaf person teaching them 'how to do their job'. Therefore, fears leading to my lack of motivation and confidence similar to the previous job came back. I survived there for two years.

In the ten years since I had left the secondary school, my negative attitude to deaf people and to my own deafness, as illustrated above, was changed almost overnight in 1989, by a book I read that had a dramatic effect on my life.

5. The last 10 years

My views in the period from 1989 onwards were completely different to what I had before then. As my attitudes toward hearing and deaf people before 1989 were based on my mainstream schooling, the tide of events since then has presented me with a choice in my perception of deaf and hearing counterparts, therefore, ignoring my views eminating from my upbringing and given to me from the mainstream background. This resulted in deaf negation and the positivity to interact socially with hearing people. One of the events that contributed to the change was from a book, 'Seeing Voices', which was brilliantly written by an American, Oliver Sacks. This was and still is my bible of the outlook in life from the Deaf perspective. The book gave an account of the hearing viewpoint of deaf people in a negative way and vice versa. This was the realisation that for the first time, after reminiscing over what happened to me over the years previously, that I had a greater burden with hearing people than I realised. Almost immediately, the feeling set in that I belonged to the Deaf World and I cursed myself for carrying the negative attitude of 'my people' over those years. As far as I can remember, it was the first time I felt resentment and anger with the secondary school that I went to years before. No matter how hard I tried to be with hearing people, social interaction with them has always been superficial with gibes, quips, banter, laughter and the odd gossip. Over the period since then I read more books written by different writers, deaf and hearing, including 'Making plans for Nigel' written by Paddy Ladd. I identified immediately with how Nigel experienced mainstreaming and realised that I was not the only one in the world by 1991. Other writings by other people such as Harlan Lane and Susan Gregory have further inspired me and strive to be with deaf people deeper. Those works changed my perspective of my own surroundings with hearing and led to better understanding of deaf people's needs.

By 1992, I entered Bradford University, as an undergraduate, to read

Peace Studies. I was blinded with enthusiasm and the welcoming attitude of both the students and staff, so I had forgotten about my suspicions of other hearing people at the University for a time. I could say that I felt more at home than at any other time with hearing people from the same course. I came to develop concepts about different kind of conflicts that faced human civilisation, which involved in political, religion, creed, ethnic and cultural divisions.

Therefore, in early 1993, I was given a task to do a project with a deafened student from the course to explore problems facing deaf people. The project, 'Deaf People in Society' had to have connotations with examples of conflict and other topics that we learnt in the course. In the investigation as part of the project, we met deaf people and hearing professionals and obtained information that we required. And there was this particular instance, where we gained our first insight into mental problems facing deaf people and I learnt some steps about social issues of deafness caused by the present day society.

This involved a visit to Richardson House in Blackburn, which was a residential clinic for mentally ill Deaf patients. The director, Frank Warren entranced us about the problems facing Deaf people, which involved in the lacking of language facing Deaf people through to behavioural problems. One of the most important was that some of the clients who attended Richardson House suffered from behavioural problems which were the result of mainstreaming in ordinary schools. For me, that was the earliest sign of awareness of deaf people in mainstream education. Warren gave us copies of published past papers and presentations made by himself, therefore some of these papers highlighted behaviour problems facing deaf people as a result of lacking social interaction. Back at the University, we made a twenty minutes presentation to the staff and students forum at the Department of Peace Studies.

We received a standing ovation for our work and it was the first time I've been positive about working in a team with another deaf student. Although, the project was finished, I did not stop there, I continued with my own private research and stumbled accidentally on a drawn graph from a page of a TALK magazine, published by the NDCS. This important graph depicted the rise of deaf children being mainstreamed and this was being overtaken by the figure showing the fall in number of those who attended Deaf schools. I put two and two together with the article of 'Making Plans for Nigel', the Richardson House business and myself experiencing mainstreaming that was there was a possibility of 64% of deaf children, by the late 1980s, could still be enduring similar treatment to that I went through?

That was not to end, by chance I visited Wakefield Deaf Centre and met a Deaf person there and I explained my concern about the issue of mainstreaming to her. She recognised that there was a deaf teenage boy who comes in from time to time who faced similar problems of social interaction with people, either deaf or hearing. She also informed me that there was a worker based at the NDCS's Family Centre in Leeds who has similar concerns as I had. So, I ended up contacting Jill Jones at the Family Centre who agreed to meet up. We shared the same concern about the problems facing ex-main-streamers and how ordinary schools could affect their behaviour as compared with those who attended Deaf Schools. By January 1994, we began to create the Deaf Ex-Mainstreamers' Group (DEX) with three other people that Jill knew. It was through publicity of DEX in journals and on television's Sign On programme that deaf people began to write to us and contacted us via meeting places. By the summer of 1994, the scale of the problem facing ex-mainstreamers and those who were still at ordinary schools was being recognised.

The pattern of the problem facing the deaf ex-mainstreamers was consistent with what I endured. DEX created social get together places for those with similar experiences at Leeds, Manchester and Birmingham from June 1994 to July 1996. During the period right up to October 1996, Jill and I made several presentations in conferences and seminars around the country. Furthermore, the members of DEX created workshops and the setting up of Deaf Befriending and Buddy Schemes with Deaf people who could act as role models for those who were still in ordinary schools. This was supported by the shared knowledge of conflict resolution made from my three years of Peace Studies. It was this undergraduate course that enabled me to under-stand the conflicts facing deaf people themselves as a result of different kind of education: the understanding of the value system as experienced by people all over the world and the importance of the typology of peoples divided by religion, race and culture, therefore facing conflicts.

This view enabled me to build an analogy faced by deaf people because of mainstreaming. I wrote a dissertation for my degree on the homogeneity of deaf people and the developing conflict between Deaf people themselves and with the hearing counterparts, using a series of analogies of other conflicts such as racial and cultural.

Another important factor which proved hearing people's social standing with me, whilst at the University, was through one month's experiment that I devised in January 1994. All my life, I've worn hearing aids to enable me to use my residual hearing, but also relied on lip-reading. This dual sensory pattern in one way or the other supported me in the understanding of hearing people's conversations.

With regard to understanding hearing people it can depend on the environment. I am best on a one to one approach with a known hearing person and worst with a group of unknown hearing peers in a noisy and dimly lit pub, for example.

Therefore, this experiment was to kill off the dual sensory pattern by not wearing any hearing aids for a month whilst mixing with hearing people. I would be left with having to lip-read harder on everyday situations. This was to see how hearing people reacted to me in their social behaviour and I to them. The result of that I lost quite a few hearing friends that way with regard to lack of patience on their part, but a few have remained in contact with me to this day. The experiment of having to lip-read people all the time, improved my lip-reading skills ten-fold.

Since highlighting the problems with both the hearing and deaf people in social interaction, there was one area that I've found comfort in. In 1989, since leaving the job working with deaf people I spent a month in the interim working as a motorcycle despatch rider around London and the Home Counties. I enjoyed it so much, being on my own with no human contact as by then I resented all human beings deaf and hearing.

That was before I read 'Seeing Voices' and became aware of my negative attitude towards deaf people and myself as a deaf person. When the 'honeymoon' period was over through to lack of work, I was forced to head back to the reprographics trade. I did go back to being a despatch rider since then for different reasons. In 1994 during the university vacation, I spent the summer in London as a long-distance despatch rider because I loved the freedom from the hearing world and did not have to face any pressure from them. Again in the summer 1996 from Bristol I was despatching all over England, but with a different. I was able to arrange to meet deaf people in various places connected to mainstreaming and managed to piece together the problems they faced in adult life.

In October 1996, I entered the Centre of Deaf Studies in the University of Bristol and by then the percentage of those mainstreamed was highlighted at 95% of deaf children. As part of the research on Deafness and mainstreaming, I had to do literature review. The review highlighted positive views about mainstreaming being better than deaf schools academically and all were written by hearing researchers. This did not say very much of the social spectrum that was facing deaf children when interacting with hearing peers, as this was not done by a deaf person.

6. Culmination gained from the effects of mainstreaming

The reader gaining the author's experience will note that since leaving school, I did my best to integrate with the hearing world socially for ten years. Those ten years was the conclusion of my personal journey gained by experience that had left me with the prospects of sitting on a fence between two worlds. The next ten years to 1999 was full of struggle to gain acceptance by the Deaf community, although I remained in the hearing world.

The changes that I've made in the last ten years were often painful and full of anger, as a result of reading the 'Seeing Voices'. In 1989, I was already working for a printing company for a few months and it was manned by hearing people and my relationship with them was already strained, despite the fact that I left a previous company run by deaf people. If I had read the book before I left that company, maybe I would have remained there with the deaf people. In 1988, I created a pressure group for motorcyclists to represent West London, which was the Motorcycle Action Group (MAG), Ealing Branch. The reason for setting that up was to improve my standing and the feeling of respect amongst motorcyclists, but it has had several drawbacks. I attended MAG representatives from other regions to monthly meetings to discuss campaign and events information to take back to the regional MAG groups.

As these were in-group discussions and I was not good at picking up the conversation, it therefore ended up with me sending in some one else who was only too happy to take down the minutes for me to read later. By the time I was running that for two years, it was the biggest group for a time in London, I was overcome with difficulties and embarrassment, with increasing awareness of what was happening to me as a result of reading the book. Therefore, I decided to call it a day and passed it on to someone else, as by then I discovered other deaf bikers. This motivated me to create National Deaf Motorcycle Club (NDMCC) with another deaf biker in 1990. The NDMCC was a tip of an iceberg for me to be gained acceptance in other areas of the Deaf community. To start off with, my signing skills were not fluent enough to make conversation, but gradually improved over the next few months and I was able to understand the gibes, quips, banter, laughter and the odd gossip eventually. Although, being with deaf bikers, I still maintained and am making new contacts with hearing bikers to this day. Therefore, I was happier with the balance of being with the Deaf and hearing world from time to time.

In the last five years, I mixed more with deaf people than with the hearing counterparts. This was the result of contacts developed through other deaf bikers, Deaf Mainstreamers' Group (DEX) and with deaf people at Bristol University and the Deaf community in Swindon. By 1999, the recognition by the Deaf community was proved by my presidency of Swindon Deaf Centre and as Chair for Swindon Signs and Sounds, which is a service users' group for deaf people living in North Wiltshire. I remained in contact with hearing people, but to a more limited extent than before, through the local motorcycle club based in Swindon. When socialising with both the Deaf community and the hearing biking club, I tend to keep the two groups on separate nights rather than mixing with them in the same pub. As for employ-ment, I tried my best to ensure that I would be with the 'right' hearing people with whom I can gain equal respect from. That is a difficult part, but I have seen hearing people working and communicating with deaf counterparts using sign language, therefore, for me that is possible to find the right workable hearing environment, but rare.

My social relationship with hearing people has improved but still is not 100% perfect. Most of the time whenever I come to be in contact with them, I have to be on guard to condition my behaviour in order to 'align' with their behavioural pattern, therefore, I could never relax easily.

Now, I could see myself the change made in the perception of the two worlds and the differences in my own judgements of myself from being negative to one of acceptance of my own deafness in the last twenty years since leaving school. If I were asked for an advice about where to send a deaf child to, I would say mainstream school, but with conditions attached. The utopian idea of mainstreaming is that no deaf child is to be left alone in the school and must have access to other deaf children of the same age. Hearing pupils and teachers must learn about deaf awareness and if possible sign language. With regard to education attainment, communication should be based on the sign bilingual approach, which involves English and sign language. Overall, based on the key points of the utopian thought, deaf children can equally enjoy with hearing people the pattern of the gibes, quips, banter, laughter and the odd gossip, as well amongst their own kind.

Adam Walker
1999

Why am I glad that I am Deaf?

I am glad that I am deaf
Because I sleep in peace at night.

I am glad that I am deaf
Because I wake up with a good feeling in the morning.

I am glad that I am deaf
Because I sleep so well through the thunderstorm.

I am glad that I am deaf
Because I don't hear anything bad or dirty from hearing people.

I am glad that I am deaf
Because I don't hear any noise anywhere.

I am glad that I am deaf
Because God gave us this special gift for a lot of good reasons.

So what is there to complain about being deaf?

Kathleen Evans
(supported by Cintra School deaf ex-pupils)
March 2001.

19 Best value review of good practice in mainstream education (2001–2004)

Presentation given at the Congress of the World Federation of Deaf People, Montreal, Canada, 2003.

Thank you for your very warm welcome to your country and to the WFD Congress. It is a great honour for our new organisation to be involved in an international conference, and to also share international experiences.

1. Deaf Ex-Mainstreamers' Group – brief background to the organisation

DEX was set up in 1994 by deaf mainstreamers and "oral" ex-deaf school pupils. We were aware of imminent language and community death in the global Deaf community because of the advent and widespread integration of deaf children in mainstream education, and the fact that DEXies do not form part of the Deaf community. The DEX Committee, staff and membership exist because of our experiences in mainstream education. We wish to see hard of hearing children being placed in resourced bilingual schools, and are particularly interested in any new ventures internationally, as there is little understanding of hard of hearing people's needs.

The new Committee originally aimed to become a support and social organisation for other deaf adults who were on the fringes of Deaf and hearing communities. DEX tried to paper over the cracks with small projects, or using our work -based projects, as we were still volunteers. As there was no real positive way of altering the effects of normalisation, we decided to become a campaigning organisation with respect to deaf education.

2. Effects of deaf mainstream education

Having collated anecdotal evidence, DEX looked for evidence of research findings. There is little concrete research on the effects of mainstream education, but the three main pieces of work are:

- Dr Peter Hindley, Peter D Hill, Sean McGuigan and Nick Kitson at St George's Medical Hospital and Springfield Hospital, London which care for deaf children with mental health problems, piloted psychiatric screening questionnaires in a group of 62 children, aged 11 -16 years, attending a residential school. The questionnaires were then used to screen a group of 93 children attending one special school and 3 units. They found a higher incidence of mental health problems amongst deaf mainstreamed children (61%) than Deaf school pupils (42%.) The conclusions were that in Deaf schools deaf children have deaf peer support, whereas most deaf children in hearing schools are placed alone, and are in an "adverse school environment and have impaired peer relationships."

- The Department of Education and Skills commissioned a literature review of all educational research in English speaking countries. Again, although largely concerned with academic achievements, there is some indication (from the largely hearing –led research) that there is little research evidence on social inclusion, although "there are sufficient personal accounts to tell us that deafness *can* lead to feelings of social exclusion." It also stated that low self concept is likely to affect academic achievement and good social adjustment and mental health are important outcomes in themselves.

- Adam Walker, MPhil, (a DEX founder) undertook to study the psycho-social effects of deaf mainstreaming for his dissertation, which is currently unpublished. One of the main findings was that 54% of the deaf ex-mainstreamed cohorts had counselling to support their negative experiences.

3. Best Value Review

DEX, therefore, decided to look at good practice. To do this we needed a methodology to measure service effectiveness. The British government implemented the Local Government Act, 1999, to develop and monitor current local government services, using Best Value targets. The over-riding concept behind Best Value is to ensure that service users' needs are met in a cost-effective way, and that users get value for money.

DEX decided to ensure the strengths of this act are extended to deaf education. In line with the Local Government Act 1999, DEX is undertaking a national Review of local authority services, using the same benchmarks as determined by the United Kingdom's government to drive through both Best Value and Quality of Life performance standards in both local government and the health services.

To achieve this we approached the Department of the Deputy Prime Minister (which is our Treasury department) and its Audit Commission for guidance. As it is always the duty of local government departments to review its own services with support from central government, Service Users do not usually conduct their own reviews. It is a first project of its kind. However, with advice, we have been able to use the principles of Best Value and Quality of Life performance measures to drive forward the project. Because time is limited today, here are just a few examples of best value principles:

- Quality of life
- Value for money
- Government accountability
- Service audit
- Performance measures – i.e. performance standards and indicators
- Sustainability – i.e. monitoring and evaluation, service maintenance and development.

Throughout the Review we will take account of the 4 C's:

- Challenge
- Consult
- Compare
- Complete

and the 3E's: economy, efficiency and effectiveness. We aim to make these principles deaf-specific.

A toolkit, used in Best Value terms, is the name for all the resources used to develop and monitor services. We, therefore, are developing a Deaf toolkit.

4. DEX Performance Standards and Deaf Toolkit

UN guidelines and UNESCO Salamanca Statement state that we have the right to "freedom of association" and to a culture and language, also, "freedom of expression" and thought and opinion. The Salamanca Framework for Action also states that deaf children should be taught in special schools or in units in mainstreamed schools. British law also protects all children from neglect and other forms of abuse, and provides civil and human rights legislation generally. DEX, therefore, devised seven Performance Standards based on British legislation and international guidelines, in addition to addressing deaf children's needs from our perspective as ex-users of the education service.

DEX was advised by government departments on Best Value, and how to achieve this. In this way, we aim to construct a Deaf toolkit, building up the tools we need to ensure that deaf children get the right education in the right environment to achieve their full potential and quality of life.

These are the Performance Standards which we hope to turn into performance indicators to be used by Local Authorities:

Deaf children's need 1: Freedom of expression, opinion, thought, conscience and religion.

Legislation and guidance: U.N. Convention on the Rights of the Child 1989, (Articles 12, 13 &14); Children Act 1989 (Section 17) and amendments; Human Rights Act 1998 Part 1 (Article 10.)

DEX Best Value Performance Standard 1: All deaf children to access Sign/English bilingualism Service Provision.

Deaf children's need 2: Freedom of association.

Legislation and guidance: U.N. Convention on the Rights of the Child 1989 (Article 15); Human Rights Act 1998 Part 1 (Article 11.)

DEX BEST Value Performance Standard 2: All deaf children to access a significant deaf peer group and Deaf culture.

Deaf children's need 3: Deaf children's access to education with hearing children.

Legislation and guidance: Education Act 1996 (Sections 316 &317 (4) (5) & (6); Special Educational Needs and Disability Act 2001 Parts 1 & 2 (Chapter 1); Human Rights Act 1998 Part 2 (Article 2); U.N. Convention on the Rights of the Child (Articles 17 & 18.)

DEX Best Value Performance Standard 3: All deaf children to have the same education as hearing peers and access to hearing children and staff.

Deaf children's need 4: Preservation of Identity.

Legislation and guidance: U.N. Convention on the Rights of the Child 1989 (Article 8.)

DEX Best Value Performance Standard 4: All deaf children to have a positive Deaf identity.

Deaf children's need 5: Leisure, recreation and cultural activities.
Legislation and guidance: U.N.Convention on the Rights of the Child 1989 (Article 31.)

DEX Best Value Performance Standard 5: Deaf children to have access to leisure, recreation and cultural activities in education.

Deaf children's need 6: Protection from abuse and neglect.
Legislation and guidance: U.N. Convention on the Rights of the Child 1989 (Articles 2, 19 and 23); Human Rights Act 1998 Part 1 (Article 17); Children Act 1989 & Amendments.

DEX Best Value Performance Standard 6: Deaf children to be protected from abuse of rights, (including the rights stated in DEX's other Performance Standards.)

Deaf children's need 7: A durable, efficient and cost effective Sign / English bilingual service with a significant deaf peer group, for all deaf children.
Legislation and guidance: Local Government Act 1999.

DEX Best Value Performance Standard 7: Establishment and sustainability of a Sign /English bilingual accommodation service for all deaf children.

5. Legal Options for parents v deaf children

Choice of educational placement

It is our understanding of the laws in our country that parents are entitled to request an educational placement for their child in the school of their choice. There may be a need to appeal, which is sometimes unsuccessful, but there is in essence, a legal option.

Informed choice of communication

In the UK, parents are told that they have an "informed choice" of communication with their deaf child, or in which language the child is to be educated. There is no law in the U.K. which states that parents have the right to choose not to allow their deaf child to sign.

This actually contravenes their deaf child's rights to "freedom of association" and also "expression". Parents do need clear and informed discussion at the point of diagnosis and beyond, but they have no right to choose anything other than a home language and /or host language *and* the native sign language, as minimum expectation.

There is much linguistic research and evidence to indicate that children need maximum exposure to language from an early age in order to become fluent. It is, therefore, clear that in order to achieve fluency in our natural language, and also in spoken language, then there can be no communication choice for parents.

This confusion over parental choice not only makes service planning problematic but it prevents deaf children from being bilingual. This is because most parents or carers of deaf children do not understand the need for their child to have access to two languages, particularly in the UK, where English is an international language and there are relatively few spoken language bilinguals.

Recently a major campaign by smaller Deaf organisations in the U.K. has led, in March 2003, to government recognition of BSL and £1m to spend, but this is only the first step in the campaign for BSL in legislation.

DEX believes that there is need for education law reform to include BSL and that it has to be carefully worded to ensure local government carries out its duties, without taking recourse to "parental choice" as a get out clause.

6. DEX Best Value Review aims and achievements

DEX wants to work with policy makers in the planning and delivery of improved deaf education.

The seven Performance Standards are wrapped around the "accommodation model" of inclusion, or enhanced resourced school which has embraced the practice of a whole school approach to Sign bilingualism, and where the whole school culture is one of Deaf / hearing biculturalism.

DEX believes that all deaf children, regardless of level of hearing loss, should attend this model of sign bilingual education.

We have visited known good practice in four Local Authorities, which were compared against three Deaf Sign bilingual schools in the U.K.

We have interviewed 64 deaf children, 30 hearing children and approx 40 parents over the four areas and Deaf schools. There are relatively few individually placed deaf children amongst these because parents did not respond to requests for permission.

DEX has also visited four Deaf schools in Sweden and two in Norway, as well as a Resource Centre there. In order to find out more about multilingualism we observed some Welsh deaf children.

We held a Challenge Event with deaf ex-mainstreamed university students, for them to comment on our work and for more feedback on their experiences.

We hope to complete the analysis of the data this year or early 2004. Our recommendations are emerging. We are in regular contact with government departments to raise our profile, and have commented on education policy issues.

7. Best Value Review findings and recommendations

Strategic planning

These are some of the main recommendations emerging from the Review:

- We aim to continue to work alongside hearing professionals who have planning, general inspection and service provision roles. As Deaf mentors of deaf children, we want to ensure that Best Value and Quality of Life (QOL) will happen in deaf education.
- BSL and Deaf enculturalisation to be incorporated into education law
- SEN Regions based on the Norway model has been recommended to the Department of Education and Skills
- Accommodation model of deaf mainstream education – significant deaf peer group within all resourced sign bilingual schools
- Parents' intervention programmes and preschool provision – Scandinavian model which we are aiming to include within legislation
- As with Scandinavian model – practice orientated educational research which links research to practice in deaf education
- Cross boundary provision for deaf mainstreamed children to attend nearest resourced schools rather than travelling long distances within their Local Authority
- Deaf children to attend primary and secondary resourced schools which feed into each other, so can remain with hearing friends.

Service provision

- For sign bilingualism to be delivered uniformly for all deaf children with all levels of deafness. New legislation should not use the term "mother tongue" as this is construed to only apply to profoundly deaf children. The inability to develop receptive spoken language is currently not reflected in the concept of sign language as a mother tongue. Research and practice in the usage of residual hearing within sign bilingualism, with or without aids is needed.
- Safety net for deaf children to change schools from mainstream to Deaf schools or vice versa, without recourse to an appeal system
- Hearing children to learn via sign bilingualism or to opt for a qualification in sign language as a subject.

- High standards and expectations essential for deaf children, in service delivery, staff training and planning and development, and including fast-track training for potentially suitable staff.

Thank you very much for your interest in our project today. I hope you have comments and questions for us.

Three Little Pigs

The first pig built a house of straw.
The wolf came.
He yelled for the pig to come out.
The pig could not hear him.
The wolf blew down the house and ate the pig.

The second pig built a house of sticks.
The wolf came.
He yelled for the pig to come out.
The pig could not hear him.
He thought it was a tornado.
The wolf blew down the house and ate the pig.

The third pig built a brick house with flashing lights and all the
    necessary deaf devices.
The wolf rang the bell and the lights flashed.
They called the zoo, using the Typetalk service.
The zookeeper came and put the wolf in a sign language class.
The wolf learnt to communicate and became friends with the pig.

Kathleen Evans
(supported by Cintra School deaf ex-pupils)
March 2001.

20 *At School* PART I

Cintra Secondary School P.H.U. Reunion
(Years 1960–1977)

The ex- pupils of the school still keep in touch via school reunions, and DEX was asked to speak in 2000. Kathleen Evans, one of the former pupils, contacted several school friends to collect their views on their mainstream experiences.

Cintra Secondary Modern School in Reading, Berkshire, was a happy school. It had a small unit for partially hearing/ deaf pupils (PHU) which about seven to eight deaf children attended every year. The deaf unit had a radio aid system, consisting of a microphone and head-phones which the deaf pupils had to use in the English and maths classes with hearing children, and so on.

Some of the deaf ex-pupils felt that they should have attended Deaf schools or have a Communication Support Worker in order that they could understand their education properly, and know what their teachers were saying. We were very much aware that we had no qualifications when we left school.

I think if deaf children cannot follow their education properly, then they should attend a Deaf school.

K.Evans

Pupil A

All my life I have lived in hearing and the Deaf worlds, but I went to a mainstream school. There were less than ten deaf children there at the same time as me. We only had a small unit in which to learn English and maths, and to concentrate on speech to improve our communication skills so that we all could get out into the hearing world able to talk. I value that very much but there also came a time when my education in mainstream was not very successful, and it would be much appreciated to have more successful achievement and knowledge.

All deaf children should go to Deaf school. Why? It is because there they can receive the same equal opportunities as hearing children. All deaf children have to work twenty to thirty times harder compared to hearing children. Most of my life I have regretted my education not being more academic through the school years.

Today I feel that all deaf children, no matter how deaf they are, should be taught by other deaf professional adults, (role models) to communicate throughout mainstream education, and a L.S.W. (Learning Support Worker) is needed. If the government closes down all deaf schools, they are not aware of the problems they are creating.

Anon.

Pupil B

I was never happy at school because I never understood what the teacher said. I was only happy in Art lesson.

Anon.

Pupil C

When I went to school I travelled by bus (two buses to and fro.) I forgot to wear my hearing aid once, so the teacher of deaf gave me a radio aid and ordered me to use it, with the headphone with microphone, all day at school even including P.E. and to swimming, as well as in the canteen. So the hearing children called to me: " You look like a newspaper reporter", etc. It was really heavy to carry all the time. They laughed at me, and I felt small.

Anon.

Pupil D

Despite being deaf from birth, I never attended the P.H.U. I had to take the radio aid around with me everywhere to every class, and give the microphone to each teacher and put the headphone on to listen to what the teachers said. It really upset me because I could not follow what the teachers said at all. But what made it worse was when the teacher of deaf ignored me completely when I explained how I felt.

During my time at school I never knew there were some Deaf schools in the UK where they provided sign language. Once a week, though, there was a speech therapist who came and taught me how to speak properly, so I felt that was worthwhile as I am now able to talk well with anybody in the hearing world.

Anon
March 2001.

20 *At School* PART II

by Alison Finch aged 13

I am shy around those who can hear better than me. I feel that if I make a mistake in front of them, it will be worst than in front of deaf and hard of hearing people. I wait for people to come to me instead of me go to them.

Before I started mainstream high school, I was the only one in my class, nearly in the whole school primary school that was hard of hearing or wore a hearing aid. When I got to mainstream high school, I realised how much more comfortable I was with deaf children than with hearing. It was lucky I landed in the form group with the deaf children as I hadn't meant to have to have been in that form. It was almost as if I had been cut off from the hearing impaired community, not that I'd ever found it difficult in primary school. I am glad I am in the form group with the deaf children in it

How I felt

I felt smaller as the conversation went on.
I couldn't hear them properly,
I shrunk back into the shadows.
Unconfident to break through and have my say
I remained quiet and put off by their laughter at
something I hadn't heard.
I felt alone with no-one to help me.

Alison Finch aged 13
24th November 1999

Bibliography

Chapter 1: Making the transition to being Deaf

Edwards J. *Language Society and Identity* (Oxford, Blackwell, 1985)

Furnham A. & Bochner S. *Culture Shock* (Taylor & Francis Books Ltd. 1979)

Higgins P. *Outsiders in a Hearing World* (Sage Publications, 1990)

Laing R.D. *Self and Others* (London, Pelican Books, 1969)

Lane H. (1983) "The Medicalisation of cultural deafness in Historical Perspective" in R. Fisher & H. Lane (eds.) *Looking Back* (Hamburg, Signum Press)

Leach P. *Babyhoood* (Penguin Books, 1974)

Chapter 4: Working through the Pain of Change.

Jones J. "Bilingualism and Deaf Identity", in Laurenzi C. & Ridgeway S. (eds.) *Progress through Equality* (BSMHD Publication, London, 1996)

Rogers C. (1961) *On becoming a person* (Constable 1995 edn. London)

Chapter 5 Part 1: Lost Deaf People and their needs

Van Cleve J. *The Academic Integration of Deaf Children – A Historical Perspective "Looking Back"* (Signum Press, 1993)

Chapter 6 Part 2: Lost Deaf People and their needs

Donne J. Poem

Finkelstein V. *Disabling Barriers Enabling Environments* (Sage Publication, 1989)

Furnham A & Lane S. "Actual & Perceived Attitudes towards Deafness" (1984), *Psychological Medicine* 14.

Gregory J. Bishop J & Sheldon L. (1991) "Language and communication", *Deafness Journal Issue* 3 Vol. 7

Jones "Bilingualism and Deaf Identity" in Laurenzi C and Ridgeway S. (eds.) *Progress through Equality* (BSMHD Publication, London,1996)

Orbach S. "Running on Empty", Article in the *Guardian* Newspaper, 24 August 1996

Storr A. *Sexual Deviation* (Penguin Books, 1964)

Van Cleve J. The Academic Integration of Deaf Children – A Historical Perspective in *Looking Back* (Signum Press, 1993)

Walker A *Possessing the Secret of Joy* (Vintage Press, 1992)

Weisel "Contact with mainstreamed disabled and attitudes towards disability: a multidimensional analysis". (ed) *Psychology* 8 No.3.A., 1988

Chapter 8: Bilingualism & Deaf Identity

Baker C. *Foundations of Bilingual Education and Bilingualism* (3rd edn, Multilingual Matters, 2001)

Berne E. *What do you say after you say hello* (Corgi, London, 1987)

Chomsky N. *Syntactic Structures* (The Hague, Monton, 1957)

Collier A. *Philosophy & Politics of Psychotherapy* (Harvester, 1977)

Crystal D. *Language Death* (Cambridge University Press, 2000)

Crystal D. *The Cambridge Encyclopaedia of Language* (Cambridge University Press, 1987)

Cummings J. and Swain M. *Bilingualism in Education: Aspects of Theory Research and Practice* (Longman, 1986)

Dashefsky Y. *Ethnic Identity in Society* (Pelican Books, 1976)

Erikson E.H. *Identity Youth and Crisis* (Faber, 1971)

Fishman J.A. *Advances in the study of societal multi lingualism* (Walter Greyter 1977)

Furnham A. and Bochner S. *Culture Shock* (Taylor & Francis Books Ltd, 1979)

Grosjean F. *Life with Two Languages. An introduction to Bilingualism* (Harvard University Press, 1984)

Higgins P. *Outsiders in a Hearing World* (Sage Publications, 1990)

Laing R.D. *Self and Others London in a Multicultural Society* (Cassell New York, 1969)

Lynch J. *Education for Citizenship* (1992)

Padden C. & Humphries T. *Deaf in America: Voices from a Culture* (Harvard University, 1988)

Rose A.N. Human Behaviour and Social Processes : An Interactionist Approach (Ed. Rose A.N.) *International Library of Sociology and Social Reconstruction* (Routledge)

Sartre J.P. *The Age of Reason* (Penguin Books, 2001)

Webster S.W. "The Influence of Interracial Contact in Social Acceptance in a Newly Integrated School", *Journal of Educational Psychology*, 52, 1985

Chapter 10: Technology

Axline V. *Dibs: In Search of Self* (Penguin Books, 1964)
Burt C. *Young Delinquent* (4th edn. University of London, 1944)
Freidan B. *The Feminine Mystique* Penguin Books, 1963)
Lane H. *When the Mind Hears* (Random House International, 1993)
Leach P. *Babyhood* (Penguin Books, 1974)
Sandstrom C.I. *The Psychology of Childhood and Adolescence* (Penguin Books, 1966)
Walker A. (1996) Bristol Dissertation (Unpublished)
Woolf S. *Children Under Stress* (Penguin Press, 1969)

Chapter 13: Cognition and Deafness

Ladd P. (1981) "Making Plans for Nigel: The Erosion of Identity by mainstreaming" in Taylor G and Bishop J (eds.) *Being Deaf: the Experiences of Deafness* (Pinter Publications, 1990).
Walker A. (1996) Bristol Dissertation (Unpublished)

Chapter 17: Deaf Community Care?

Dalby D. *Linguasphere Observatory* (Hebron, Wales)
Morrison T. *Playing in the Dark. Whiteness and the Literary Imagination* (Harvard University Press, 1992)
Edward D. Said *Culture and Imperialism* (Vintage, 1994)
A Service on the Edge (1997) Social Services Inspectorate Report
Walker A. (1996) Bristol Dissertation (Unpublished)

Chapter 19: Best value review of good practice in mainstream education

Hindley P., Hill P. D., Mc Guigan S. and Kitson N. Psychiatric Disorder in Deaf and Hearing Impaired Children and Young People: a Prevalence Study, *Journal of Child Psychology and Psychiatry.* 1994, vol.35, No. 5 pp. 917–34
Powers S., Gregory S., The University of Birmingham and Thoutenhoofd, E. D. The University of Durham (eds.), *The Educational Achievements of Deaf Children – A Literature Review* Research Report No. 65, DfEE